KU-748-245

GREAT DINING DISASTERS

Charles Neilson Gattey

Illustrations by ffolkes

Columbus Books
London

To Patricia and John

ACKNOWLEDGEMENTS

The author wishes to thank in particular Sir Geoffrey Jackson
for permission to quote from his unpublished reminiscences;
also the publishers for quotations from *Nicole Nobody* by the
Duchess of Bedford (W. H. Allen), *Pray Silence: a toast-
master's story* by Ivor Spencer (Robert Hale), and *The Most of
S. J. Perelman* (Simon and Schuster); the literary agents John
Farquharson Ltd for *The Moon's a Balloon* by David Niven
(Hamish Hamilton); and Mr Christopher Driver and Mr Drew
Smith, past and present editors of *The Good Food Guide*, for
extracts from the 1982 edition.

British Library Cataloguing in Publication Data
Gattey, Charles Neilson
    Great dining disasters.
    1. Dinners and dining—Anecdotes, Facetiae,
satire, etc
    I. Title
    394.1'5   TX737
    ISBN 0-86287-092-5 Pbk

Copyright © 1984 Charles Neilson Gattey

First published in Great Britain in 1984 by
Columbus Books
Devonshire House, 29 Elmfield Road, Bromley, Kent BR1 1LT

Phototypeset by Tradespools Ltd, Frome, Somerset
Printed and bound by Butler & Tanner Ltd,
The Selwood Printing Works,
Frome, Somerset BA11 1NF

CONTENTS

Horror stories for gourmets   1
The gourmet duped   10
One man's meat   12
Coward in the kitchen   20
Blighted breakfasts   22
A fortunate calamity   24
Dropped bricks at dinner   25
The everlasting egg   34
Mutiny in the kitchen   36
Cooks in the soup   40
Cook's revenge   45
When butlers bite   46
Pink sauce   55
The perfect footman   56
Shopping à la française   59
Thirteen at table   60
What the eye doesn't see   62
What the carver couldn't do   68
No dress for dessert   71
Etiquette outraged   72
When the house is on fire   74
James Barrie entertains   75
Lunching over the stables   77
At the captain's table   78
Dogs' dinners   79
Pets at the table   82
Dining with duke and duchess   84
Banqueting with the Lord Mayor   88
Eating with royalty   90

Dining with the President   99
'Pray silence . . .'   101
Putting one's foot in it   107
After-dinner entertainment   112
Escaping gas   115
Feasting on the film set   117
When bare bosoms shocked   119
Where Eve dared not tread   121
Snubs for snobs   122
Are outsized Eves dangerous?   124
Stealing and swopping   126
Childish behaviour   129
The offending artichoke   131
Indian pudding   132
Many a slip   133
When food isn't what it seems   136
Embarrassing encounters   138
The waiting game   141
The rebellious customer   144
Greasing the palm   147
Welshing customers   149
A cod-piece for the audience   152
The morning after   153
The lady vanishes   156

Horror stories for gourmets

For those with a palate dining out can often prove a disappointment.

The menu itself may well be a work of fiction.

'"Turbot, sir," said the waiter, placing before me two fishbones, two eyeballs, and a bit of black mackintosh,' complained Thomas Earle Welby in *The Dinner Knell*. Edmond de Goncourt, describing a dinner at Zola's, wrote in his *Journal* for 3 April 1878 that one of the guests, the novelist Alphonse Daudet, compared the flesh of the grouse to that of an old courtesan's 'marinated in a bidet'. And in his novel *Something Happened* Joseph Heller lamented that in the United States nowadays: 'You can't get good ice cream anymore. It tastes like gum and chalk.... You can't get good bread anymore even in good restaurants (you can get commercial rolls) and there are fewer good restaurants.... Butter tastes like the printed paper it's wrapped in. Whipped cream comes in aerosol bombs and isn't whipped and isn't cream.'

Working wives often lack time to cook. 'I'm afraid your dinner is a little overdone this evening,' apologizes one such harassed individual in a cartoon as she sets a burnt offering before her beloved. 'What!' he exclaims. 'Have they had a fire at the fetch-and-carry?'

Could it be that their lamentable eating-habits cause our national leaders to make the wrong decisions? Napoleon Bonaparte ate irregularly, hastily, and without any interest in what he shovelled into his mouth. Some of his worst defeats occurred when he was suffering from indigestion.

Gerald Ford, the former American President, ate the same lunch day in and day out, disclosed John Hersey in the *New York Times* – a ball of cottage cheese over which he poured a small pitcherful of A1 sauce, a sliced onion or a quartered tomato, and a small helping of butter-pecan ice-cream. 'Eating and sleeping,' he told Hersey, 'are a waste of time.'

The same newspaper reported on 19 June 1974, when Ford was Vice President, that in his speech to the Grocery

Manufacturers of America at their convention in White Sulphur Springs, Virginia, he assured them of his 'particular affinity' for the makers of instant coffee, instant tea and instant oatmeal. 'I happen to be the nation's first instant President,' he said. 'I only hope that I prove to be as pure, digestible, and as appetizing to consumers who did not have a chance to shop around for other brands of Vice President when I was put on the market.'

Horror stories for gourmets

John Cheever in *The Wapshot Scandal* castigates average Americans for eating as though under siege and unable to obtain fresh food. Meat, fried potatoes, peas and so on were all bought frozen – and the only flavour the potatoes had was that of soap! 'It was the monotonous fare of the besieged ... but where was the enemy?' They were their own enemies, of course.

*   *   *   *   *

Gourmets are understandably apt to be intolerant of poorly prepared food. Sir William Rothenstein at one of his own dinner parties was devastatingly critical of the fare served at a friend's table.

'But poverty is his skeleton in the cupboard,' Lady Rothenstein said tolerantly.

'Still, he needn't bring it out and put it on the table for dinner,' retorted her husband.

*   *   *   *   *

One disaster gourmets sometimes have to face is the discovery that their favourite dish at a particular restaurant has deteriorated in quality. Many years ago such a lover of fine fare complained to mine host of the Old Ship in Brighton that the turtle soup lost its savour after being on the menu for several days.

The other confided: 'As you are an old customer, sir, I'll be frank and admit that when the demand exceeds the supply, we are obliged to – well, how shall I put it? – stretch. Turtle soup with us has, like the year, four seasons. The first day, it is fresh and strong: that's its spring. The second day, we throw in a little cayenne to make it more piquant: that's summer. The third day, we strengthen with extra forcemeat and catsup: that's autumn. The fourth day we "stretch" with aqua pumpo: that's its winter.'

*   *   *   *   *

Serving the wrong dish at the wrong time of year can get the chef into trouble. Louis Eustache Ude was one of the French chefs responsible for raising English cooking standards in

3

the first half of the last century. For a while he was employed by the Earl of Sefton and then became the chef of Crockford's where he committed the crime of serving grouse out of season, for which offence the horrified Marquess of Queensberry had him prosecuted. *The Times* published an account of Ude's sparring with the magistrate, and made fun of his broken English:

M. UDE: I know nothing at all about vot vent into de room. I never sawed it at all.

SIR F. ROE: Whether you know it or not, the Act of Parliament makes you liable.

M. UDE: Upon my honour, dat is very hard. Ven I got de summons I remonstrated with my Lord Alvanley, and he say, 'Oh, never mind, Ude, say dey vere pigeons instead of grouse.' 'Ah, my lord,' say I, 'I cannot do better than call them pigeons, because dat bird is so common in his house.'
(Loud laughter.)

Sir F. Roe, who appeared greatly to enjoy the scene, said he should certainly pay the lowest penalty, namely, five shillings.

M. UDE: Vell, I shall pay de money, but it is dam hard.

Next day in Crockford's a suspicious-looking salmi was served to the Marquess, who asked peremptorily for the menu to be brought to him. The waiter ran to Ude, who wrote one out, calling the dish '*Salmi de Fruit défendu*'. The haughty Marquess could not help but laugh.

*   *   *   *   *

S.J. Perelman, in his story 'The Saucier's Apprentice', entertains us with a plot to ruin the *renommée* of the cuisine at Maxim's which had arranged to export five of its sauces to the United States. Distrusting American cooking methods, Maxim's flew their own experts over to New Jersey to supervise the final stages of preparation and guard against any tampering – such as thickening with flour.

Perelman meets Marcel Riboflavin of the Sûreté who reveals that the head of their Bureau Culinaire had reported 'a perfidious assault on the very citadel of our national cuisine' – the detection of flour in a pipkin of *sauce béarnaise* served at Maxim's in Paris itself. The crime had come to light through a valued customer, the Comédie-Française tragedian Isidor Bassinet, complaining that the sauce served him was more suitable for calking a boat. Then, two evenings later, the gourmet Greek shipping tycoon Satyriasis was celebrating his silver wedding anniversary there with his wife and his mistress; all the dishes proved superb till they tried the salad and found to their horror a canned pear stuffed with cream cheese and walnuts, garnished with cole slaw and Russian dressing. This gastronomic outrage caused Satyriasis to pass out.

It was then that Riboflavin arrived on the scene and tried to find the culprit. But this only made the latter perpetrate worse indignities, serving customers such items as fried clams encapsulated in deep fat, mashed potatoes 'pulsating with marshmallow whip' and baked grapefruit.

'Forgive me for underscoring the obvious,' Perelman tells the detective. 'Surely it must have occurred to you that a woman, and patently an American, was at the bottom of all this?'

In reply, Marcel reveals that, with the management's co-operation, he disguised himself as an assistant pastry chef and worked in the kitchens of Maxim's where he became suspicious of a girlish youth and later hid in the wardrobe of 'his' bedsitter and surprised 'him' when 'he' had stripped down to 'his' brassière. Overcome with remorse, Gristede Feigenspan weeps and confesses that she is a feature writer for *Effluvia*, a periodical circulated free by American supermarkets, and that the purpose of her impersonation had been to introduce American dishes to the patrons of Maxim's and establish the culinary pre-eminence of her country.

'I take it she paid the inevitable price for her audacity?' Perelman commented.

'That is a matter of opinion,' Marcel replied, with an enigmatic smile. At that moment a young woman approached, whom he introduced as Gristede, now his wife. She invites Perelman to dinner and he stammers: 'I – er – I'm just en route to Beirut. I mean I'm off to a fiesta in Trieste –'

'Don't be an Airedale,' she interrupts. 'We'll give you a real home-cooked meal. Hasn't Marcel told you about my noodles Yankee Doodle, smothered in peanut butter and mayonnaise?'

Perelman looked at Marcel, but his face, 'flies and all', had turned to stone. He had shut up like a clam.

*   *   *   *   *

Max Boyce, the Welsh entertainer, once appeared on an Australian TV chat show with a Greek restaurateur who proceeded to cook a special dish in an electrically-operated pan. Unfortunately, the thermostat did not function and the mixture was slow to cook. Taking advantage of a break for commercial advertising, the Greek asked Boyce to eat some of the stuff when they came on again. He did as requested, but could not swallow it because the principal ingredient turned out to be squid, which was barely cooked and rubbery. So he kept it in his mouth and the moment the programme ended, he turned aside and spat it all into his palm. No sooner had he done this than the Greek rushed up to thank him and in seizing Max's hand to shake it managed to cover his own with the nauseous concoction.

As a result, no doubt, of this television appearance, a Welsh woman called on Boyce and brought him a homemade faggot to remind him of his native land. She also took the touring Welsh rugby squad one each. The following day, the Welsh team was beaten, and a newspaper report stated baldly that the players had been seen with 'faggots' before the match. The prurient assumed the worst and blamed the defeat on sexual delinquency.

*   *   *   *   *

In the 1930s, when British television was in its infancy, Marcel Boulestin would demonstrate the art of cookery for fifteen minutes every fortnight from a cramped studio. Once he was preparing a flat omelette which, when he tossed it into the air, failed to come back – much to the astonishment of the viewers. Alexandra Palace was besieged with phone-calls. Had the omelette stuck to the ceiling? No. The explanation was simply that the camera had failed to follow the toss.

*   *   *   *   *

Horror stories for gourmets

James Beard, the American cookery expert, was once preparing a soufflé live on television when he realized that his hoped-for masterpiece was not going to rise, so to save his reputation he whispered to his assistant, 'Drop it on the floor!'

*   *   *   *   *

John Fothergill in *Confessions of an Innkeeper* relates how he was taken to an hotel on the Quai Voltaire in Paris to eat *bouillabaisse*. According to him, it was a pale, sloppy, fishy affair, full of bones, and whilst picking his way amongst them he told his friend, 'A man eating *bouillabaisse* is like an ass looking for a wisp of hay in a bushel of needles.'

Cats, however, are not so fussy. A Parisian owned a black Persian which had round its neck a collar bearing her telephone number and its name. One evening she was rung up and a voice asked: 'Do you own a cat called Mimi?'

'Yes, I do – but why?' was the reply.

'This is the Café Neptune. Mimi has drowned herself in our *bouillabaisse*.'

*   *   *   *   *

The state of the kitchens in some catering establishments does not always satisfy government inspectors. One of these guardians of public health was distressed to find dirt, dust and cobwebs everywhere in the rear part of a café.

'Just look at that table!' he pointed out. 'Why, the grime is so thick I could write in it!'

'So you could,' replied the cook, 'but you are an educated man.'

The inspector snorted. 'And what does this mean? There's a fly at the bottom of each one of these tea-cups?'

The other shook his head and answered, 'I'm not a fortune-teller.'

*   *   *   *   *

An old restaurant off Wall Street that had been in business ever since 1872 kept under glass a ham and cheese sandwich prepared on opening day. When the relic was eighty-four

7

Great Dining Disasters

years old, a new cleaner, unaware of this, thought it was time the display case received attention and took it away for that purpose, placing the historic sandwich on a clean plate. A busy waiter then served it to a customer, who, when the mistake was discovered, was rushed to hospital.

'Why all that fuss?' grumbled the man. 'It tasted just like every other sandwich I've eaten in that joint!'

*   *   *   *   *

An Englishman who was a stickler for cleanliness sat at a table outside a café near the Place de l'Opéra in Paris and ordered some soup. When it arrived, there was a fly afloat in it. He beckoned furiously to the waiter and, pointing, complained: '*Regardez* – *un mouche!*'

As the waiter removed the fly with a spoon, he superciliously corrected the other's French: '*UNE mouche, monsieur.*'

'Good heavens!' the Englishman exclaimed. 'What marvellous eyesight you must have to spot its sex!'

The gourmet duped

Not all gourmets have the finely perceptive palates of which they like to boast. Chavette, owner of the restaurant Brébani in Paris, suspected that the well-known journalist Monselet, who claimed to be an expert in gastronomy, did not really have much sense of taste, so one day he invited him to dinner.

According to the menu, the fare consisted of swallow's-nest soup, brill, izard cutlets and capercaillie, together with various fine wines. Monselet rhapsodized over every dish, much to the growing contempt of his host, who at the end revealed that the soup was a purée of noodles and kidney beans, the brill merely cod, the izard just lamb cutlets marinated in bitters, and the capercaillie in fact a small turkey sprinkled with absinthe. As for the wines, the Clos-Vougeot was a *vin ordinaire* to which had been added a spoonful of cognac and a violet flower, and the Tokay a Macon plus a few drops of punch.

Some years later Monselet was invited to a luncheon party at the home of Joseph Favre, author of the *Grand Dictionnaire de cuisine*, who was also a gifted cook. The journalist was very late, arriving at four o'clock when Favre and the other guests had finished the meal. However, as the latter had been let into the secret and wanted to witness Monselet's reactions, they joined him at the table and ate a second luncheon. The menu consisted of burbot liver *en caisse, saucisson de Lyon* with Isigny butter, *escalopes de saumon* with tartare sauce and new potatoes, and *omelette à l'ambre-gris*, followed by dessert.

As Monselet ate he commented like an expert gastronome upon the merits of each course, with especial praise for the omelette. When the second sitting was over, Favre confessed that it was all a hoax. He revealed that in order to study the nervous system of crocodiles the distinguished physiologist Paul Bert had imported some from Egypt and he, Favre, had attended the dissection of the reptiles; Bert retained two brains and half a tail for himself and gave Favre a whole one, together with four brains and six eggs almost ready for laying.

The shocked journalist now learnt that those 'burbot

livers' he had called exquisite were crocodiles' brains, the salmon escalopes in which he had detected a Scottish flavour were the reptiles' tails, while the *omelette à l'ambregris* was made with their far-from-fresh eggs. To add to Monselet's dismay, Favre further disclosed that the butter was margarine and the *saucisson de Lyon* mere horsemeat sausage.

* * * * *

The year 1870 was an ill-starred one for gourmets in besieged Paris and the ingenuity of chefs was stretched to the limit in trying to cope with alimentary scarcities. Large as the elephant is, it would have needed several times the number of such animals in the capital's zoo to have provided the meat to fill all the popular elephant pies that the hungry citizens devoured. It was a tiny bone found in one that provided the clue: almost all the contents came from mice.

Rats, too, helped to sustain the Parisians during those disastrous days. The flesh of well-fed ones in the wine cellars of the Gironde was once used for *entrecôtes* by the coopers, who after skinning and cleaning them grilled the rodents over a wood fire and ate them with olive oil and shallots. This was how the *entrecôte à la bordelaise* originated.

One man's meat ...

Not only in restaurants but in some homes is it true that the meat one man could not chew becomes another's tasty croquette.

Poor quality is one reason why eating out can turn out to be a disaster rather than a delight. Laura, Duchess of Marlborough, has written of her parents' visit to Golden-eye, the Jamaican home of the Ian Flemings – 'a house where the food was well-known to be sparse and often inedible'. One day at lunch the cook-housekeeper brought in a Pyrex dish containing what looked to the Duchess's famished father like toad-in-the-hole *du pays*. He poked resolutely through to the bottom, attempting to scoop out what he thought were two sausages. Then, as his spoon touched them, they wriggled away: those plump brown objects were really the servant's fingers grasping the almost empty dish.

*   *   *   *   *

The precept that when abroad one should do as the natives do sounds admirable, but may prove an ordeal in practice. W.C. Hunter, an old resident of Canton during the years 1825–44, penned some amusing verses about an Englishman in China apprehensively tasting a bit of one dish, then a little from another. But he brightened up...

> And he thought himself in luck
> When close before him what he saw
> Looked something like a duck!
> Still cautious grown, but, to be sure,
> His brain he set to rack:
> At length he turned to one behind,
> And pointing, cried: 'Quack, quack?'
> The Chinese gravely shook his head,
> Next made a reverent bow:
> And then expressed what dish it was
> By uttering 'Bow-wow-wow!'

*   *   *   *   *

One man's meat . . .

Great Dining Disasters

Lady Diana Cooper was another diner confronted with food she did not care for at a banquet given in her honour by a sheik in North Africa. It consisted of 'half a burnt sheep, schlocky puddings eaten with wooden spoons, then artichokes smothering what we've got used to calling somebody's feet'.

* * * * *

The food that delights one nation can often disgust another. The traveller Gordon Gaskill relates how in Africa he met an elderly Englishman who talked about his experiences and the shock of one culture meeting another for the first time.

'Can you imagine,' he asked Gaskill, 'people so primitive that they love to eat the embryo of certain birds, and slices from the belly of certain animals? And grind up grass seed, make it into a paste, burn it over a fire, then smear it with a greasy mess they extract from the mammary fluid of animals?'

While Gaskill shuddered at such barbarism, the man went on: 'What I have been describing, of course, is a breakfast of bacon and eggs and buttered toast.'

* * * * *

The celebrated American playwright George S. Kaufman had such strong prejudices where food was concerned that hostesses would usually phone him or his wife in advance for approval or alteration of their dinner menus.

One evening Edna Ferber, his collaborator for such plays as *Dinner at Eight* and *Stage Door*, invited Kaufman and Beatrice, his first wife, to a dinner party, but failed to consult either of them about the food. There were many other guests that Sunday evening and the meal began with a hot cheese *hors d'oeuvre*. Cheese of any kind being anathema to George, the sight and odour of this made him hold his napkin over his mouth and nostrils lest he became ill. Bea, to avoid a scene, surreptitiously removed what was on his plate.

Edna Ferber could not have selected anything that George detested more than the next dish – roast goose with a thick gravy and all the trimmings. The last straw was a roquefort dressing on the salad. Thoroughly disgruntled, he prepared to leave, but Bea held his arm and whispered that she would eat it all for him, which she did.

Fortunately, the sweet and coffee pleased Kaufman. At last the moment came for leaving the table and Bea was so relieved that the ordeal was over that she rose and moved away with nervous haste. Unfortunately for her, the buckle of her evening gown had caught in the lace tablecloth when she leaned over her husband to remove the spurned food, and as she moved away cloth, china and silver were dragged off the table and crashed on to the floor.

Kaufman stared at the shattered débris and then told Edna: 'That's what I call pulling off a few good ones.'

*   *   *   *   *

Norman Longmate, in his book *The GIs*, describes the eating habits of American servicemen in Britain during the Second World War. Their tastes varied: those from the south liked cornmeal bread and 'black-eyed Susans' (the seeds of the cow-pea, white with black spots) but northerners would not touch either. All GIs, however, liked eating sweet and savoury foods together. When their British hosts invited them to Sunday lunch they were startled to be asked for jam or syrup with which to coat the Yorkshire pudding. Porridge would be requested for pouring on the steak, apricot jam for the pork pie; fried bacon and eggs were smothered with strawberry jam and clotted cream, fish cakes with marmalade, hamburgers with jelly, and beetroot with condensed milk. (Perhaps the British had forgotten that back in the eighteenth century the great Dr Johnson had poured lobster sauce over his plum pudding.)

Among unpopular British foods, sausages and sprouts were at the head of the GIs' list. An American flight engineer in Suffolk claimed that British sausages contained a mere 20 per cent of meat, the rest being cereal. Though this was true, largely due to rationing restrictions, the sausages were certainly better than the German kind – which were mostly sawdust. As for the loathed sprouts, in the office of a group commander of the First Bombardment Wing was a notice that read: 'If you must make a forced landing, do it in a brussels sprouts patch.'

Widely circulated among the GIs was a document entitled

15

Great Dining Disasters

Guide to British Technique at the Dinner Table that pointed out how the table manners of the host country differed from the Americans' own. Viewed from a distance, the Englishman eating looked much like 'a drummer in a jazz band hitting a one-piece swing'. He kept his fork in his left hand and never transferred it to his right as Americans did, which enabled him to maintain a ceaseless rhythm between his plate and his mouth. Throughout the British Isles the sons of Uncle Sam were trying to master this complicated manoeuvre, which was not easy.

'It calls for the development of a completely new set of muscles in the left hand as well as a new sense of timing and co-ordination between the shoulders, elbow, wrist, fingers and mouth,' wrote the author of the guide:

> It is amazing how easy it is to miss your mouth when you first start, and also how miserable a fork full of brussels sprouts feels in the ear when the hand has missed its target. But in the cause of Anglo-American unity, the GI Joes all over these islands are doing it. In an effort to do my bit towards co-operation, I have been eating that way myself of late and have reached such a point of dexterity that Londoners sitting near me in a restaurant move to another table for fear of being hit by food fragments when my stomach tells my mouth that zero hour is at hand.

It is only right that Britishers visiting the States should return the compliment by eating in American style. The UK Ambassador was once invited by President Coolidge to breakfast with him so that they could discuss complicated clauses in a trade agreement. The diplomat was shocked when his host poured his cup of milk into a saucer, but thought it tactful to follow his example. The President gave a slight smile but made no comment as he bent down and placed his saucer before a grey cat waiting hopefully under the table.

*   *   *   *   *

Tastes in food vary not only from nation to nation but from class to class. The late David Niven, when mess officer for the Highland Light Infantry, managed to buy a quantity of the finest caviar from a Russian ship, and on that evening, as a surprise treat, he arranged for it to be served at general mess. To his disappointment, the caviar failed to be received with shouts of approval. Instead, there was much grousing among the men. Eventually, Niven asked a sergeant the reason.

'It was muck,' he snapped. 'Cook must be drunk – blackberry jam stinking of fish!'

*   *   *   *   *

To a sensitive restaurateur nothing is more distressing than to find an unappreciative customer ruining the taste of a dish prepared by a first-class chef. John Fothergill recalls in *Confessions of an Innkeeper* his horror at seeing a businessman lunching in his restaurant pick up a bottle of Lea & Perrins' sauce and pour some into his soup. He went up to the fellow, greeted him, then remarked with a pleasant smile: 'The next time you intend coming here, I wish you would telephone me beforehand, then I would make some special soup for you out of blotting-paper so that you could flavour it yourself.'

*   *   *   *   *

The saying 'One man's meat is another man's poison' can also apply to the kind of women preferred by their opposite sex. Speke, the nineteenth-century explorer, tells us that the King of Karalwe (in Africa) fed his wives entirely on milk, to keep them as fat as possible. They had to drink it all day, through straws, and were whipped by a eunuch if they desisted. The diet evidently worked, for these unfortunate women could only tumble about like seals in their huts.

Nowadays women in the West commonly go to the other extreme. In the United States, for example, those members of one weight-watching club who have failed to shed any surplus pounds have to wear grotesque pig-patterned aprons and sing, 'We Are Plump Little Pigs Who Eat Too Much Fat, Fat, Fat!' To get rid of it (and to learn what and what not to eat) the ladies play such games as 'Calories Baseball', in which the pitcher shouts out 'Carrots!' or 'Nuts!' or 'Dates!' and so on, together with appropriate weights, and the player in to bat has to bawl back the correct calorific values.

All this effort does not always succeed in its purpose. As

one woman said to a friend: 'I haven't lost weight since I've been counting calories and carbohydrates, but my arithmetic has improved.'

In today's highly competitive world of showbusiness lightweights usually win all the prized roles. Even in opera the heavies are no longer tolerated. A critic exulted when Lily Pons started the new trend: 'At last a Carmen who weighs less than the bull!'

Critics, too, can suffer from a weight problem. One such was Alexander Woollcott, known for his wounding wit. Now and then he would go on a diet.

A playwright encountering a friend said: 'I hear "Old Vitriol and Violets" has dropped 40 lbs.' The other enquired, 'On whom?'

*　*　*　*　*

Despite the modern preoccupation with one's weight, there are still some who opt out. Beneath the picture of the food writer James Beard which hangs in Charley O's bar is the quotation: 'A gourmet who thinks of calories is like a tart who looks at her watch.'

*   *   *   *   *

Sometimes men entertain the women they are hunting at restaurants where the menu is bed-sized and the food is always cooked to perfection. In 1952, when Elizabeth Taylor was divorced from her first husband, Nicky Hilton, the millionaire Howard Hughes invited the star to dine at a Beverly Hills haven for gourmets in the hope of persuading her to marry him next.

Once they were seated, he had the *maître d'hôtel* read aloud to her the colourfully phrased descriptions of the dishes, making comments of his own after each in order to show off his knowledge of food: 'From the Midi, a great way of serving eggs', 'Only one restaurant in Budapest serves a goulash to match this', 'You won't taste better kebab anywhere in Greece', and so on.

Having paid avid attention to all that was said, Elizabeth declined every suggestion and instead asked for a hamburger, adding, 'a great American dish from all over the United States.' Then, noticing how devastated the *maître d'hôtel* now looked, she went on, 'and a portion of french fries.'

Coward in the kitchen

When Noël Coward started living at Spithead Lodge, Bermuda, he found it impossible to engage a cook so he and Cole Lesley learnt to fend for themselves. It was August and not only hot but very humid, and one morning when Noël was on his own he wore nothing but the daily cleaner's plastic apron which was patterned with rosebuds. Suddenly, a most respectable-looking man knocked at the kitchen door. He apologized for doing so but said it was because he had rung in vain at the front of the house. 'I am the Bishop of Bermuda,' he announced.

'How do you do,' said Noël. 'Just give me a moment to see how my vol-au-vent cases are getting on.' He then bent down to examine them, exposing to the visitor the full expanse of his bare bottom, surmounted by a bow. When he turned round, the Bishop had rushed out, never to return.

Coward became such an excellent chef that summer that when asked to write a foreword to his friend Adrianne Allen's cookbook, *Delightful Food*, he did so willingly. He wrote: 'Among the trends of the present day ... far and away the nicest is the trend towards the kitchen ... but I am sorry to say that it wasn't until lately that I heard the call to come into the kitchen.'

That year, 1956, had been an eventful one for him, and not the least eventful part had concerned his culinary adventures. There was the wonderful day when his soufflé rose to such heights that it hit the top of the oven, which he watched 'open-mouthed' through the glass door. He had spent thirty-six hours trying to make puff pastry, for which he had cancelled all engagements and his sleep. Then there had been ...

> the night the Oven Blew Up, the afternoon the lid flew off the Water Mixer and sprayed unreachable parts of the ceiling with chocolate mousse and the day I said, 'Leave the canapés to me', and later found that several of the guests had taken one nibble and then dropped them, not I must admit without reason, behind the sofa. I am learning the hard way but I am proud to say that at the end of my first year I have more than once turned out a creditable three-course dinner for six.

Noël goes on to say that up till that year he had always

appreciated good cooking but never learned to cook. The only pronouncement he had ever made on the subject was, 'If it's rissoles, I shan't dress', a rule he made in 1925 and to which he always strictly adhered.

Blighted breakfasts

It is 7.30 am in the early days of this century and at the far ends of a long table in their Boston home sit Judge John Lowell and his wife. They have been married for some forty years and as usual he is busily engaged reading the *Law Report* and quite oblivious of her presence. Never before has she dared to ask the question she now nervously utters: 'John – is there anything interesting in your paper today?'

The Judge stares over his spectacles at the little woman. 'No, of course not,' he replies and, returning to his reading, does not notice the agitated entry of the maid who hurries to Mrs Lowell and, in trembling tones, conveys to her the alarming news that cook has burnt the Judge's cereal and, worse still, that there is no more in the pantry.

This is no minor misfortune, for throughout the whole of their married life Mrs Lowell has made it her first task every day to see that her husband is fortified for his legal duties with oatmeal for breakfast. 'John!' she calls. 'There isn't going to be any oatmeal for you this morning.' She waits in trepidation for him to explode with wrath.

The newspaper is lowered and the Judge's face confronts his wife. 'Frankly, my dear,' he says with a smile, 'I never did care for it.'

*   *   *   *   *

Another husband, the Marquis of Blandford, a cousin of Lord Randolph Churchill, enjoyed most of all bacon and eggs for breakfast, so great was his dismay when one morning he lifted the cover of the silver dish which usually contained them and found instead a tiny baby doll. It had been placed there by his wife so as to let him know she had found out that he was the real father of a new addition to the family of their friend Lady Aylesford.

*   *   *   *   *

Breakfast, like any other meal, can be marred by disagreeable company. When Sir Winston Churchill was staying one weekend with his cousin, the Duke of Marlborough, at

Blenheim Palace, the other guests were Waldorf Astor and his wife Nancy. She and Winston argued with increasing acrimony on every topic that was discussed until on the Monday morning Nancy snapped: 'If I were married to you, I'd put poison in your coffee.'

Churchill retorted: 'Nancy, if I were married to you, I'd drink it.'

*   *   *   *   *

When one is accustomed to enjoying a certain food for breakfast, it can be irritating to find that it has been purloined. Never very well off, Lady Diana Cooper had no scruples about taking what she wanted from rich friends. After a visit to Lord Rosebery's country home, she asked him to tell his chauffeur to take her and a friend to a railway station several miles away at a very early hour. Just before departure Lady Diana slipped upstairs, then hurried back with something wrapped up in a paper bag which she hid inside her coat as they went out to the Rolls.

Once in the train, Lady Diana's companion ordered breakfast but the other borrowed a plate instead and took out of the bag the fine kipper which the footman had left on a tray outside Lord Rosebery's bedroom door.

A fortunate calamity

Sometimes a cooking calamity can have happy consequences. The celebrated Antonin Carême had an ancestor
who was Pope Leo X's chef and who once delegated the
cooking of a stew to a pupil. The youth placed the meat in a
pan without adding stock and butter as he should have done
and then left it over the fire. As a result, the fat in the meat
started burning. Aghast at what had happened and fearing
Carême's fury, he hurriedly poured the stock over it all and
prayed that his blunder would not be noticed. The experienced chef, however, on inspecting the stew, remarked at
once on its uncustomary colour and sampled some to try and
detect the cause. To his relief and pleasure, he found it had a
delicious flavour, and asked the quaking underling how he
had achieved this. After preparing some more meat himself
in the same way, he decided to use this method for the
future, and other chefs soon followed suit.

Dropped bricks at dinner

If, as a host or hostess, you are to become celebrated as a laughing-stock, you should make no attempt to remember the names, backgrounds or tastes of your guests. Instead, you might emulate the legendary Miss Evans, who invited fifteen to dinner but addressed all the envelopes to the same person; on another occasion, when dining out at a friend's, Miss Evans became confused and, imagining she was at home, addressed the whole table, including her hostess, saying, 'This food is foul. What has upset my cook tonight I simply cannot think.'

To attain a similar notoriety as a guest, it is as well to cultivate a memory like the proverbial sieve. The writer Alice Duer Miller woke up one Saturday morning with an awful feeling that she had failed to turn up at an important dinner the previous evening. Hastily she consulted her diary, which proved her guilty. Her immediate impulse was to ring up and apologize. Then she changed her mind. Better put it in writing and send flowers? No, that was too ordinary, not worthy of an inventive writer. At last, she had an inspiration. The following Friday, elegantly gowned, exactly a week late, she went up the steps to her hostess's front door and rang the bell.

It is important, of course, at formal dinners not to be correctly attired, like the octogenarian who turned up at a grand dinner with his trousers gaping open in front. When his hostess took him behind a potted palm and drew attention to this, he merely laughed, then assured her: 'Madam, dead birds do not fall out of their nests.'

*   *   *   *   *

To start off on the wrong foot, you ought to say something outrageous on arrival, but there is always the danger that your host or hostess will be too preoccupied to listen to you. A journalist once claimed that at Hollywood parties it does not matter what you say because no one ever listens to anything anyone else is saying. To test his theory, he once told his film-star hostess: 'I'm sorry to be late but I strangled my wife.'

She responded with her parrot cry of 'Swell, swell!' not having paid the slightest attention to him.

If you are a woman guest and want to be regarded as a *femme fatale*, you might wear white kid gloves daubed with crimson so you can scare off eligible men with the story that you have just bumped off your fifth husband and nothing will remove those damned spots.

*   *   *   *   *

The absent-minded have been known to put letters into the wrong envelopes, with devastating consequences. Emerald Cunard liked to relate how Lord Curzon once sent her two notes, one an invitation to dinner and the second clearly meant for another woman but slipped by accident into the same envelope.

The latter commenced: 'My beautiful white swan, I long to press you to my heart...'

*   *   *   *   *

Once at a dinner in Dunraven Castle, after the ladies had retired, Lord Turberville remarked to a gentleman present that the 'old trout' who had been seated on his right was the ugliest woman he had ever seen. The other replied: 'I'm sorry to hear that you think my wife so unattractive.'

Hastily the peer said: 'Oh no, sir, I've made a mistake. I meant the lady on my left.'

The man frowned, then told him, 'Well, she is my sister.'

'Your sister!' repeated Lord Turberville, staring hard at his guest. 'Then, if what you have said is true, I must confess that I've never seen such an ugly family in all my life.'

*   *   *   *   *

The foot-in-mouth remark has enlivened many a dinner party. One host told his guests, as his wife disappeared into the kitchen: 'The little woman cooks for fun. For a good meal, we go out to a restaurant.'

After visiting Oxford to attend a matinee of one of his plays, William Douglas Home joined his wife who had gone ahead to the house of some friends where they were to dine.

Dropped bricks at dinner

On leaving, their host said to the playwright's wife: 'Thank you, Rachel, for a lovely dinner.'

'What do you mean?' William asked, puzzled.

'I brought it from home as their cook was off,' she explained.

'In that case,' replied Douglas Home, 'I am at liberty to say that the fish was the most disgusting thing I've ever eaten.'

Their host forced a smile, and said: 'That was the only dish I provided.'

*   *   *   *   *

Shyness can also be the cause of unpopularity at dinner parties. A young man was once seated next to a formidable-looking lady who made him so nervous that he could not eat or talk. Presently she observed: 'What a tiny appetite you have!' And he, desperate to please her with a compliment, stammered: 'To sit next to you would make any man lose his appetite.'

*   *   *   *   *

Sitting next to gargantuan Viscount Castlerosse might have put some fastidious women off food. The slim Nancy Astor at a luncheon patted his enormous stomach and jibed: 'If that was on a woman, we would know what to think.'

To which he replied: 'Well, it *was* last night, so what do you think?'

*   *   *   *   *

Laura Corrigan, the American who became one of the most colourful of London hostesses, was noted for her malapropisms. James Lees-Milne recorded in his diary for 24 June 1944 that when he dined with her at Claridge's she had said of Lord Londonderry: 'Charlie has three balls on his cuisse.'

*   *   *   *   *

A dowager duchess at a banquet was appalled to see the man opposite her turn the silver equestrian trophy before him upside down and examine the hallmark with a magnifying

27

glass. His wife, noticing the dowager's expression, shrieked across the table, 'Has a eye for quality, has my treasure. Why, if he thought you were valuable, he'd turn you up and see if you were marked.'

Their hostess could not resist pointing out, 'I won that for one of my jumpers.'

'So you're a champion knitter!' exclaimed his wife.

*   *   *   *   *

Sir John Gielgud has admitted that he is prone to dropping bricks. Being invited out to lunch so often has on occasion confused him, and once at a fashionable restaurant he was telling his host how much he disliked Mr X when someone came up and greeted his host by name. He was Mr X.

*   *   *   *   *

When one is accustomed to alcoholic refreshment, if only occasionally, staying with friends who do not keep any in the house can be a strain. Sir George Leveson Gower describes in his reminiscences a visit to Sir Stafford Howard, whose wife was strictly teetotal. Howard had advised Gower when he invited him to bring what he needed and keep it hidden in the bedroom. Grateful for the suggestion, Sir George arrived with a large flask of whisky and a siphon of soda with which he refreshed himself in secret after lunch and dinner.

One day Lady Howard remarked to her husband that she feared their guest must be unwell as he always retired to his room following a meal. Sir Stafford tactfully explained that George had to take a tonic.

'But why doesn't he keep the bottle on the sideboard, which would save him the trouble of going upstairs?' Lady Howard asked.

Sir Stafford suggested: 'Well, I fancy that he thinks it might ruin our appetites if we saw him taking medicine in the dining-room.'

'How charmingly considerate of him,' Lady Howard cried approvingly. 'I *do* think that nice!'

*   *   *   *   *

Dropped bricks at dinner

An inebriated guest can spoil a dinner party. Princess Elizabeth Bibesco one evening at Emerald Cunard's chattered away in an increasingly loud voice during the meal, then, after the coffee, she suddenly slumped on to the table. Emerald beckoned to the butler and said: 'Her Highness has fainted. Give the Princess a little brandy.'

The butler replied in a carrying whisper: 'Her Highness has drunk all that was left in the decanter since the soup.'

A somewhat similar situation occurred when Lady Diana Cooper gave a luncheon party in the South of France. Present was an almost destitute Russian princess. She had not eaten and drunk so well for years, and eventually, being very intoxicated, she slipped off her chair and slumped on to the carpet. Always the perfect hostess, Lady Diana immediately got down on her hands and knees and curled herself up next to her guest.

'It's much cosier having coffee on the floor,' she told the other with a reassuring smile.

*   *   *   *   *

To be late for a luncheon or dinner engagement can wreck a friendship or a business deal. The routine excuse 'I was tied up' is likely to irritate your host or hostess unless, like Lady Diana Cooper, you are able to add, as she could on one unfortunate occasion, that masked burglars with designs on your jewels and furs had done just that.

*   *   *   *   *

Eva Perón was delayed by a hostile mob waving their fists and shouting: 'Puta! Puta!' when she was on her way to a banquet with General Franco in Madrid. After explaining why she was late, Eva asked: 'Why did they call me a whore?'

Franco replied: 'Never mind, dear Señora. I've been retired for years but they still call me a General.'

*   *   *   *   *

Even the best-intentioned guest can give offence. The late Joyce Grenfell had some friends who inherited a large,

29

dilapidated Victorian house. Painstakingly, floor by floor, they restored the place, keeping it in period. When all was finished, their friends were invited to a party in celebration. As the guests filed into the dining-room, one of them paused on the threshold and cried, 'I say, you're going to have fun doing up this room!'

*   *   *   *   *

Being abroad and out of touch for some time can increase your chances of dropping a brick. For instance, you might tell a risqué story about a Mrs Fitzsimmons-Smith only to find out that following a divorce and a face-lift she is now the Countess of Cowes and seated next to you. Sir William Hayter related how during his stay in Cairo as British Ambassador Sir Miles Lampson became Lord Killearn. A few months later, the new peer and his wife entertained to lunch a woman who said, 'It's wonderful that you're here now and not those Lampsons everybody disliked so much.'

*   *   *   *   *

Even professional diplomats make the occasional gaffe. Lord Curzon of Kedleston used to relate how he dined early one evening at White's when the only other member sitting at the long table asked him what he was doing that night. Curzon replied that he was going to see a play called *Diplomacy* for the second time, something he rarely did. His questioner revealed that he, too, was going there, but for him it would be the 87th time. Curzon was astonished and told him that he did not consider the play or any of the cast deserved such a compliment. Before the two men parted, the stranger said: 'By the way, my name's Coghlan.'

'Coghlan!' Curzon exclaimed, now realizing with dismay that he had been talking to the actor playing the leading role.

*   *   *   *   *

Perhaps the worst thing any guest can do is to damage or destroy one of his hosts' irreplaceable possessions: spilt wine can ruin cherished carpets, awkward gestures shatter Meissen, and so on. When Sir Osbert Sitwell first went to

30

Dropped bricks at dinner

New York, he was entertained by a celebrated picture-collector and his wife. They were most hospitable and after dinner the latter took him to see a wooden chair, 'a cross between a camp-stool and a shooting-stick'.

'This is our Dante chair,' she said.

'You mean Dante sat in it?' asked Sir Osbert.

'No, he was asked to, but refused,' the proud owner replied, 'and that is why we call it our Dante chair. I want you to sit in it on this, the night of your arrival in New York.'

Great Dining Disasters

Flattered by the honour thus being bestowed upon him, Sitwell complied, but hardly had he done so when the chair crumbled into dust. 'Crumbled,' he declares, 'is not the word to describe the process, since it carries no sense of immediacy, while this disintegration was instantaneous.' Despite the seriousness of the disaster, Sir Osbert says that his hostess behaved admirably, betraying no sign of the distress it must have caused her.

*   *   *   *   *

Before the Cultural Revolution, there lived in Shanghai a rich Chinese whose home was exquisitely furnished. One evening he entertained an American businessman to dinner, and beforehand showed him his treasures, chief of which was a beautiful Ming horse, five feet high. 'There are only four of these in existence,' he disclosed with a satisfied smile, adding that according to all the experts its value was so immense as to be practically incalculable, but in any case he would never part with it.

During the meal, the American over-indulged himself and became extremely drunk. Shouting that he was 'going for a ride on that horse' the man threw a leg over it before his horrified host could intervene, lost his balance and fell on to the floor, smashing the porcelain to pieces.

The owner sighed and, bending down, helped the wrecker to rise. 'Do not worry yourself about this accident,' he insisted. 'It makes the three remaining horses that much more valuable.'

*   *   *   *   *

For personalities very much in the public eye, dinner invitations are common occurrences, and many have to be declined. This can lead to embarrassment on occasion. Dame Nellie Melba used to decline invitations by telegram, but to save money would devote much time to deleting unnecessary words. As a result her message often could not be understood by the recipient, who would have to wire back asking what she meant.

One day Dame Nellie decided to use the phrase 'touched thought' in future as an abbreviation for 'touched by your thought'. This led to an unfortunate incident. A letter arrived from an Australian woman visiting London in which she invited the diva to dinner that evening. Accompanying the letter was a huge basket full of orchids.

'I certainly shan't dine with her,' Melba told Beverley Nichols, then her secretary. 'She's one of the people who say I drink. Send her a telegram – "Regret indisposed".'

Nichols asked if the woman ought not to be thanked for the orchids. Melba snorted: 'You can add – "Touched thought". It'll all come into twelve words.'

And that was the message sent over the 'phone. Unfortunately the operator must have been hard of hearing for the telegram delivered to the scandalmonger read: 'Regret indisposed. Touched port.'

The recipient dined out on it for weeks.

* * * * *

Those anecdotes should suffice to give the reader ample guidance on creating a refreshing discordance at dinner parties. Sometimes, though rarely, disaster at the dining-table has been positively courted. Six men once arranged that, for amusement, each should invite as his guest to a dinner the man he considered the most unpopular in London. When the day came and they all gathered for the occasion, only one guest turned up: the Liberal statesman Sir William Harcourt, who besides being Gladstone's chief supporter had an arrogant manner and a withering wit. He solved the puzzle by saying: 'I must say, I think it is uncommonly nice of you fellows to invite me, but why did you each take the trouble to write me a separate letter?'

* * * * *

In London in the 1920s, a hard-up but lively and handsome young man-about-town gained a name for giving a dinner party almost every week. He went to considerable trouble to find out when his affluent friends and acquaintances had engagements which it was impossible for them to put off, then he would invite them to festivities he had no intention of holding. Thus he came to be regarded as a generous host, was constantly being invited back – and never failed to accept such hospitality.

The everlasting egg

Sir George Sitwell was a great eccentric responsible for some bizarre inventions. His son, Osbert, relates in *Left Hand, Right Hand* how, one summer in London, he was summoned urgently to father's bedroom. After locking the door, the old man lowered his voice and said: 'You know I sometimes have an idea with money in it.' Then he continued with a cackle: 'I've just produced an egg.' He paused to watch the effect this startling claim had on Osbert, and, satisfied with the look of astonishment it produced, he revealed: 'It's a breakfast egg. The yolk will be made of smoked meat, the white of compressed rice, and the shell of synthetic lime – or a coating of lime. It will be delicious, will last forever, and be ready at any time. It wouldn't matter where you might be, in the desert or on a polar expedition, all you'd have to do would be to boil it for two or three minutes, as you wish – and there would be your breakfast, ready for you, and very nourishing and sustaining. You'd feel wonderfully fit after it, ready to do a real day's work.'

To humour Sir George, Osbert suggested that he ought to patent the idea forthwith. The inventor replied that was why he wanted to consult his son. Could he suggest how best to market it and make some money? He himself thought Selfridge's were the best bet, as they seemed very go-ahead. But whom should he approach, and how should he announce the reason for his visit? He dare not entrust his egg to anyone else lest it be stolen.

'I should ask for Mr Gordon Selfridge himself,' advised Osbert. 'Tell the commissionaire to take you up in the lift, and just step into Mr Selfridge's sanctum, saying: "I'm Sir George Sitwell, and I've brought my egg with me."'

The baronet regarded the suggestion favourably, and thanked his son profusely. Next morning at eleven, wearing a silk hat and a frock coat and clasping a bundle of papers with diagrams on them, he left for Selfridge's in Oxford Street. He was very late for lunch on returning and though his eyes seemed to rest on Osbert with a certain coldness, he never disclosed what had transpired during the interview – if it had taken place. His wife tactfully did not enquire, and he never mentioned it again.

The everlasting egg

35

Mutiny in the kitchen

In Victorian times the cooks at great houses who prided themselves on their culinary competence often objected to amateurs from upstairs trespassing in their territory. Lady Beatrice Violet Greville in *Vignette of Memory* relates how as a 15-year-old girl she stayed with her aunt, a rich widow who owned a beautiful house in Herefordshire. One day Lady Beatrice was informed that cookery lessons were being held in Hereford and she was to attend them. On her return, she was asked what she considered herself capable of cooking as a result of the tuition. She replied that she hoped to be able to manage puddings.

The novice was solemnly ushered by the butler into the spacious kitchen, replete with pots and pans. There she was introduced to a grand cook in cap and apron, surrounded by her minions, waiting beside the large, glaring fire. Lady Beatrice shyly explained that on her aunt's orders she had come to make a pudding.

The required ingredients were immediately presented to the intruder, who with trembling fingers drew out her notes and, under the cook's sarcastic gaze, started to prepare the mixture. When Lady Beatrice had finished, the cook offered to boil the pudding for her. Having been made miserable by the woman's unfriendly manner, the girl eagerly accepted and escaped upstairs, thankful her disagreeable task was over.

At lunch, with great solemnity, Lady Beatrice's effort was served on a silver dish. She hardly dared to look at what she feared would be an unholy mess, instead of which a delectable-looking pudding appeared. Her aunt tasted it and pronounced a verdict of 'Excellent!', to which all the guests agreed. Their hostess smacked her lips and called for a second helping. Then came a catastrophe. She took a spoonful and a moment later cried: 'A pin – a pin in the pudding! I might have choked and died!'

Recalling the humiliation this caused her, Lady Beatrice wrote how unfortunate it was that 'this accursed pin' should have fallen to her aunt's share. 'One of the guests might have picked it out and laid it quietly beside her plate, but my aunt – no – this was a case of lèse-majesté. "Is this your pin?" she glared at me. "That nearly killed me!"'

Mutiny in the kitchen

The cook, of course, indignantly denied all responsibility, and no one in the kitchen would admit blame. Thus came a bad ending to previous joy, commented the beginner from upstairs.

*   *   *   *   *

Cooks have always needed humouring. A childless couple were shattered when a splendid one gave notice after only a month because she had been seduced by a soldier and was expecting a baby. Rather than lose their treasure, they agreed to adopt what turned out to be a boy. A year or so later the cook confessed that she had slipped up again, and this time it was with a sailor. Her indulgent employers in return for her remaining also adopted the daughter that was born.

All seemed well until one day the cook came once more in a flood of tears to her mistress. 'Don't tell me you've fallen for an airman this time?' cried the latter.

'Oh, no, I've learnt my lesson!' cook replied, 'I'm going 'cause four of you is too much work.'

*   *   *   *   *

When the First World War broke out, Mrs Cornelius Vanderbilt had the German Ambassador to Washington, Count Bernsdorf, staying with her in Newport. Not expecting hostilities to break out she had already arranged to hold a large dinner party in his honour. By the date in question Belgium and France were being over-run by the Kaiser's armies and Americans, according to their ancestry, were taking sides in the conflict.

Mrs Vanderbilt assumed that the Count would have enough tact to find an excuse for leaving her earlier than planned. To her dismay, however, he failed to do so, thinking no doubt that his departure would be interpreted as an admission of his country's guilt. In desperation, she phoned those other friends who had not put off coming and asked them to take the greatest care not to mention the War during the dinner.

But Mrs Vanderbilt had failed to take into consideration the feelings of her staff, who all came from England and the invaded countries. The meal commenced without any contretemps. Soup was served. Then no one came to remove the plates though the hostess kept ringing. At last an agitated Swiss chambermaid arrived and gave her mistress a note. It read:

> We, the undersigned, regret to inform you, madam, that we cannot any longer serve the enemy of our respective countries. We have thrown the rest of the dinner into the dustbin and we have all left your service. There is nothing else to eat in the house. We hope you all enjoyed the soup, for we took good care to spit well into it before it went to the table.

The letter was signed by all who worked in the kitchen. The dinner party ended abruptly and the Ambassador departed early next morning.

* * * * *

Another Newport society function, in the 1890s, ended even more disastrously. Delmonico's of New York, entrusted with the catering, had prepared a superb collation for the guests. Ward McAllister in *Society As I Found It* relates how after dancing an outdoor cotillion in the twilight, the guests went hungrily in to eat, only to find that the inebriated coachmen and grooms had locked the French waiters in the cellar and, taking over the dining-room, had eaten every mouthful of solid food. They drank all the champagne and left untouched the ices, jellies and confectionery. So their employers were forced to return home to dine.

'The coachmen swayed to and fro like the pendulum of a clock,' says McAllister, 'the postillions ... hung on by the manes of their horses when they lost their equilibrium. The women, as usual, behaved admirably. As one said to me: "My man is beastly intoxicated, but I shall appear not to notice it. The horses are gentle, they will go of themselves."'

* * * * *

A strike at the home of the late Joshua Cosdens was given one of the longest of all newspaper headlines by the first Cholly Knickerbocker, the celebrated New York journalist. Maury Paul, who coined the phrase 'Café Society' (and once said: 'Nobody gives a damn who you sleep with – it's who you're seen dining with that counts').

The headline ran: 'COSDENS' SERVANTS STRIKE IN MIDDLE OF DINNER LEAVING COSDENS' GUESTS FACE TO FACE WITH STARVATION OR WHAT IS WORSE FACE TO FACE WITH THEMSELVES.'

Cooks in the soup

Many a cook in the past has begun her life in domestic service as a kitchenmaid, including the writer Margaret Powell. Her first engagement as a cook was brought to an abrupt end by some redcurrant jelly.

Having never made any jam, let alone jelly, she could not get it to set despite hours of boiling. Eventually, in desperation, she melted several sheets of gelatine in the mixture. Then it set so hard that when she dropped some on the floor, it bounced. So, she confesses in *Servants' Hall*: 'As the redcurrant jelly made by some previous cook was nearly all gone, I thought it would be better if I wasn't there when my concoction was opened.'

* * * * *

Whilst hygiene is very important when preparing food, it can be overdone. An investigator visiting a cathedral-city restaurant reported in a recent edition of *The Good Food*

Cooks in the soup

Guide: 'Home-made vanilla ice was plentiful, over-sweet, and nicely flavoured with Domestos.'

Another food-sampler, this time of an Essex restaurant's cuisine, found the French beans had 'a strong taste of coffee'. Could the *commis* chef have spilt some while drinking a cup – or was the washing-up to blame?

Culinary incompetence is not a rare commodity, as other reports reveal. In the West Country the 'Mushrooms *arménienne* was a mixture of thin, gravyish liquid, frowsty mushrooms, stale walnuts, bits of unpeeled tomato, celery and a few bits of bacon. It was no surprise to find that exactly the same brew was used at the next stage to top the veal *maison*.' At a Scottish hotel the 'Gruyère fritters were five rocky balls with a solid, bread-pudding filling tasting of oregano rather than Gruyère, orange-yellow in colour ... A horrible dish.' At another hotel, the 'Venison St Hubert was unsalted, re-heated, overcooked and pappy, in the same all-purpose brown sauce that afflicted other main dishes we tried. Long-frozen, we thought.' And in a West End restaurant, 'everything that wasn't tinned or frozen was pickled in malt vinegar, and most of the staff should have been'.

*   *   *   *   *

Sometimes the best food is retained by cooks for their own consumption, and receives most careful preparation for the table. In Victorian times, it was often alleged that the food in the servants' hall was better than that served above-stairs. A *Punch* cartoon shows a kindly butler telling his mistress: 'Steak a little hard, ma'am? We've a particular tender leg o' lamb in the hall – shall I enquire if you can have a slice of that, ma'am?'

*   *   *   *   *

Nowadays, good cooks are scarce and the IQ of some novices rather low, as in the case of one engaged by a Las Vegas housewife.

'I want you to dice these beets for dinner,' she told the girl.

Two hours later, the new cook complained: 'I cut up all the beets, but putting black dots on them is driving me crazy.'

*   *   *   *   *

Great Dining Disasters

Writing in *The New Yorker*, S.J. Perelman described in 'Kitchen Bouquet' how he once engaged an eccentric character, Philomène Labruyère, to cook for him. Every night she would barricade herself in her bedroom armed with a sixteen-inch steak knife. All she gave him for dinner was meat loaf and cold fried chicken. Tiring of this monotonous diet, he was about to dispense with her services when he discovered that she came from Martinique, so he saw that she got to know that he would 'look tolerantly on fried plantain, yams, and succulent rice dishes'.

Perelman was delighted one afternoon to detect signs that Philomène was preparing for his delectation a West Indian feast. From the kitchen came the scents of saffron, pimento, and allspice and the sound of calypsos, and occasionally he spied the bright bandanna which the cook, clearly in a happy mood, wore on her head. In order to be appropriately attired for the gourmet meal he expected, Perelman donned whites and cummerbund and indulged in several stengahs before seating himself at the dining-room table. Shortly afterwards, Philomène sailed in bearing a salver on which lay the wing and under-carriage of a chicken accompanied by two slices of meat loaf – all of them repellently cold.

For some minutes, Perelman was too stunned to move, then, summoning up all his courage, he made for the kitchen. The sight before him outraged his duped stomach, for there sat his 'black hibiscus blossom' enjoying *potage parmentier avec croûtons*, a crisp *gigot*, a *salade fatiguée*, and *pot de crême au chocolat*.

'You – thing,' said Perelman, though at some length, and five minutes later Philomène was travelling back to St Pierre.

After this disheartening experience Perelman engaged a male cook called William, a gaunt Australian who called himself a 'raw-fooder', believed cooking killed food, did not know the meaning of 'pot' roast, maintained that his employer could become three times as virile by eating ferns, and was able to prepare bran in a hundred different ways, 'each more ghastly than the last'. Surprisingly for so committed a vegetarian, he devoted his spare time to polishing and whetting his set of steel carving knives.

William's preoccupation with those knives and the fact that his employer happened to be reading an account of the gruesome Lizzie Borden case aroused a certain apprehension in the American's mind. It deepened when, coming down for breakfast on 4 August (by a strange coincidence the 47th anniversary of the Fall River disaster), Perelman saw laid out on the table precisely the same kind of fare which had been served on Second Street that catastrophic morning – heated-up mutton soup, cold mutton and bananas. Thoroughly scared, he wrote out a note terminating William's employment, added a reference and a cheque, and left them in a prominent position in the man's room before concealing himself in the woods until he was certain that the cause of his disquiet had departed.

Perelman's dream cook by now was a stout, motherly soul who so loved preparing food that her hands were always covered in flour while a hot apple pie forever cooled on the windowsill. He put a detailed advertisement in the papers hoping to attract such a person, but eventually he had to make do with an old Latvian woman, Ilyeana, who joined him in such a hurry that he suspected she might be on the police department's 'wanted' list. The way she carried on in the kitchen supported this feeling. Then, a week later, a newspaper clipping fell out of a letter she had received from Canada. Perelman picked it up. His attention was arrested by the heading 'MISSING MAN BELIEVED FOUND'. Below this, he read that the Mounties dragging a lake in Saskatchewan had recovered some parcels containing the cut-up body of a man. They were seeking his sister, believed to be in Latvia, to assist them in their enquiries.

Perelman questioned Ilyeana about the report, taking care to station himself by the nearest defensive weapon, the fire tongs.

'Ah, this happen every time I get good job,' she sighed. 'Always pickin' on me. Well, I guess I go up there and take a look at him. I know that head of hair anywhere.'

At the station Ilyeana bought a ticket to Savannah, which Perelman thought a very roundabout way back to Canada.

* * * * *

The demon drink has seduced many a cook. Barbara Hulanicki in her engrossing reminiscences *From A to Biba* relates how she and her associates took over the dilapidated Derry & Toms department-store building in Kensington High Street, London and transformed it. They engaged to take charge of the huge Rainbow Room and fifth-floor banqueting rooms a stout little French chef with a genial face topped by a striking red wig. He impressed his employers with his piles of laudatory press cuttings, his authorship of two books on catering and his knowledge of the art of gastronomy. He even insisted on their sampling dishes at restaurants so that they would learn by experience what he was talking about.

A firm had been chosen as overall building contractors and to celebrate the signing of the agreement it was decided to hold a buffet lunch for about fifty people in the office which would also serve as a test of the new chef's ability. He agreed to prepare snacks and canapés of such excellence that they would become the talk of the town, and so that his demands regarding equipment could be met a temporary kitchen was installed as the old ones were still being renovated.

The top brass from the building contractors and their lieutenants assembled in the office for a pre-prandial drink, and after a while word came from the commissariat that the gourmet glories were taking longer than expected to prepare. When an hour and a half had passed without their being served, Barbara's husband Fitz went to investigate. Returning with grim news about the wonder chef, he took his wife aside and told her: 'He's pissed.'

'What about the food?' Barbara enquired.

'There's two girls frying sausages on a primus stove,' was the discouraging reply.

At last the food appeared. It consisted of the thickest of thick sandwiches and stale rolls, each stuffed with a couple of half-cooked, tough sausages. The building contractors' managing director tackled a roll heroically and grunted with relief when eventually his teeth sawed through to the sausage – only to become stuck in it. Refusing to be eaten, this poked out of his mouth with its mate, from which it had not been detached, swinging below and scattering tomato sauce down that immaculate white shirt-front. The other members of the firm were experiencing similar trouble and from all around came exclamations of dismay.

Then, at the height of this disaster, the intoxicated chef emerged, with his toupee awry and his beaming face covered in sweat, foolishly expecting congratulations. Fearful that an even worse second course threatened, the guests fled.

Cook's revenge

In his autobiography Godfrey Winn recalls a story related to him by the 91-year-old Somerset Maugham when Winn was staying with him at the Villa Mauresque. Alleged to be the only plot Maugham had never used, it concerned a Spanish woman who loved her son 'with such a primitive, possessive passion that when he committed a crime and was sent to prison it did not lessen her feelings, and on his release she welcomed him back home and slaved for him'.

Then, to her fury, she found out that he was infatuated with a girl she considered totally unworthy of marriage to the son she worshipped.

This mother was a first-rate cook, and her son never left a scrap on his plate.

'Did you enjoy your meal?' she enquired one day.

He replied that he had, and thanked her.

'Then let me tell you what you have eaten,' she said. 'It was the liver of the girl who tried to steal you away.'

Maugham concluded his account by revealing that this grim story was based on fact.

When butlers bite

There have been employers who could be mistaken for their butlers. Lord Curzon towards the end of his life remarked despondently to his second wife, 'I look more like a butler out of place than ever, and am sure that when we are turned out I can easily get a good situation.'

In fact, he not only resembled a superior sort of butler but behaved like one, organizing and supervising every detail of a dinner party, even writing out the names on the place-cards and the menus for meals in the servants' hall.

When Viceroy of India, he spent much time investigating the misdeeds of his cook and wrote in triumph to a friend that they had caught the man redhanded. 'He returned 596 chickens as having been consumed within a single month. We went to the tradesman who had the contract and found the figures were 290.'

Butlers themselves can look the part and yet disappoint in practice. An American millionaire's widow married an Italian Count over twenty years younger than she was. Having to return to the States on business, she left her sexy Adonis in their Riviera villa. It was the first time they had been apart since the wedding and the day before her departure a new butler arrived.

'This is Rushmore,' she told her husband. 'He will not only wait on you during my absence but he'll cook, too.'

A week later, the Count had an old crony in to dinner. The food served was a gastronomic disaster and the guest asked: 'Why does a gourmet like you put up with it?'

'I'm sorry,' the grass widower replied, 'but Rushmore is here to try and cook my goose. I've discovered he's a dick in disguise.'

*   *   *   *   *

Butlers serving the old aristocracy were so well-trained that they remained impassive no matter how great a disaster might occur, their speech restricted to the clichés of their calling. For example, when the Black and Tans raided Dunsany Castle, the butler enquired as they left: 'Whom shall I say called?'

The usual way of getting rid of unwelcome visitors is to tell them that the master or mistress is absent or indisposed. In the latter case, it is best not to specify the ailment. Once, when a friend called on Lady Holland, her butler told the man: 'You cannot see her Ladyship as she is in bed with sciatica.'

'Another of those damned Italians!' growled the caller.

When Sir Winston Churchill instructed his butler to tell a certain bore that no one was in, he added: 'And to convince him, smoke one of my cigars when you open the door.'

*   *   *   *   *

Great Dining Disasters

In the 1920s and '30s, one of the most colourful of English hostesses was Mrs Ronnie Greville, called by her intimates Maggie. She was the daughter of the rich Scottish brewer McEwan and his cook-housekeeper and her country home was Polesden Lacey in Surrey. She inherited McEwan's fortune and from him financial acumen and drive as well as a cruel wit. An excellent mimic, she loved to entertain her guests with a savagely satirical impersonation of Lord Simon asking her to marry him (and chewing the poker when she turned him down).

Mrs Greville had two eccentric butlers, Boles and Bacon, who were invariably drunk when she had dinner parties and whom she would rage at but never dismiss. Boles, who was in her employ for 42 years, looked like the stage version of a perfect butler and behaved like one if sober, and she left him a considerable sum in her will. Bacon, in contrast, was squat, had the red face of a heavy drinker and told everyone he was a Communist. Kenneth Clark in his autobiography described what happened one day when he lunched at Polesden Lacey. Baby tongues, the most celebrated dish in his hostess's repertoire and normally prepared only for royalty, were to be served in Sir Kenneth's honour.

Seated at the end of the table, he could see what was happening behind the screen placed before the serving hatch.

As the delicacies came up from the kitchen, Clark saw Bacon eyeing them greedily. Then, giving way to his desire, the butler seized the baby tongues and started cramming them into his mouth. Despite his speed, the delay in serving the dish was at once apparent to Mrs Greville, who asked Boles what had become of the baby tongues. With true below-stairs *esprit de corps*, he came to the rescue of the culprit, explaining: 'There were none to be had in the market this morning, madam.' Meanwhile, Bacon hurriedly fixed a napkin over his bespattered shirt to conceal the clues to his crime, and carried in the next course.

Bacon's misbehaviour reached its most monstrous when Sir Austen Chamberlain and his daughter Diana came to dinner. Lord Boothby, also a guest, recalls that the butler was obviously sozzled. After he had almost spilled some soup over Diana, Mrs Greville sent for a footman, asked for paper and pencil and wrote, 'You're drunk. Leave the room immediately,' adding her initials.

48

The footman gave the note to Bacon, who studied it in a fuddled daze, scratched his head, and, putting the piece of paper on a silver salver, handed it to Sir Austen. When the latter read the message, he was so astounded that his monocle fell out and he remained silent for the rest of the meal. Mrs Greville was extremely upset by the incident, but surprisingly she did not sack Bacon.

Great Dining Disasters

Even when the butler is reliable, the writing of such notes can cause trouble. A certain hostess who always kept a watchful eye on everybody at her dinner parties once scribbled a message and told the butler to deliver it to a lady at the far end of the table. The latter, who had not brought her glasses with her, asked the Member of Parliament on her left to read the message aloud. It went: 'My dear, please do me a favour and don't neglect that man on your left. I know he's an awful bore, but talk to him.'

*　　*　　*　　*　　*

During the Edwardian era Mamie Fish's splendid luncheon parties at Crossways were celebrated in New York high society, and not to receive a repeat invitation was regarded as a social disaster. This was the fate of Bobby Van Cortlandt and when, after a considerable lapse of time, he ran into Mamie at another party his acerbic opening gambit was: 'Never can remember what you call your house, Mrs Fish. Isn't it Cross Patch?'

She retorted: 'Never mind – it's a patch you'll never cross, young man.'

Mamie had a first-class cook and the most highly regarded English butler in the United States, Morton. Well over six feet tall, he presided over her meals with impressive formality. His alert, searching gaze would instantly detect the slightest violation of the rules of etiquette. He could punish the worst offenders with a single haughty stare. As this paragon told everyone, he had served only English dukes until then. If Mrs Fish dared to try to interfere in his duties he would reply: 'Just as you wish, madam, but I must point out it is not done in the best English households.'

On one occasion, to his abhorrence, Mrs Fish yielded to the request of some *nouveau riche* friends and loaned them Morton to grace their dinner party. The wife exasperated him by buzzing about him like a wasp as the table was set out. He had reached the end of his tether when she started instructing him as to which wine to serve with each course, but he held his tongue until she reached the Apollinaris water.

'I hope you know how to serve that – you won't make any mistake?' she asked him.

Morton's response was devastating: 'Madam, I have had the care of some of the most esteemed cellars in Britain. Apollinaris water should be boiled. I have always seen it boiled.'

With age, what were once regarded as amusing idiosyncrasies can become tiresome and eventually intolerable, and so at last Mrs Fish reluctantly decided that the time had come for her and Morton to part. She was unwise enough to give him his congé the day before a dinner party to which a considerable number of guests had been invited. He retaliated with Machiavellian cunning by painstakingly unscrewing his employer's entire gold dinner-service into over three hundred pieces, which he left in a well mixed heap on the dining-room floor. The other domestics proved incapable of reassembling the service, so Mrs Fish in desperation telegraphed Tiffany's in New York. Two of Tiffany's staff dashed out to Newport and managed to complete the necessary work just before the guests were due to sit down to the meal.

There were many in New York society whom it pleased to hear of this near-disaster, for Mamie Fish had become increasingly autocratic and tactless in her remarks. She greeted one guest with, 'Oh, how do you do? I had quite forgotten I asked you,' and a crowd of them with, 'Make yourselves perfectly at home – and believe me, there is no one wishes you there more heartily than I do.'

When the season started at Newport and the women she had not seen for months were seated for dinner, she once told them: 'Well, here you all are again with older faces and younger clothes.'

When she condescended to dine for the first time with another *nouveau riche* acquaintance and was told proudly, 'This is my Louis Quinze salon', she retorted, 'Oh, and what makes you think so?'

*   *   *   *   *

Sir Geoffrey Jackson, the British Ambassador to Uruguay who was kidnapped by terrorists and held prisoner for eight months, also served as a diplomat in Egypt, where he and his wife had some amusing experiences with butlers. He told me how in war-time Cairo his wife's first formal menu was meant to be sumptuous but simple, built round a saddle of the local lamb. 'She was already a prodigious cook, but the rule for the foreigner was that the basics must be left to the cook-houseboy. As cooks go ours was good, though an even better butler. He was a *Dinka* from the Sudan, some six-foot-six of slender Nilotic elegance, and as vain as a peacock.'

The guests arrived but not, in its turn, the dinner. 'There in the kitchen was our Hassan poised on a stool, with an Armenian tailor plus a mouthful of pins fitting him for a new suit, for which he slowly revolved as the ankle-length *galabiya*, or robe, was draped around him for length. It was in a bright ginger, hairy tweed with a bookie overcheck. The effect was both spectacular and horrible. So, too, were my comments.'

Even so the soup was all right, so Sir Geoffrey was by now on his mettle for his first official carving. 'At last, in came Hassan, by now towering in natural shantung crowned with a new turban. In his hands, he bore our largest silver tray – a wedding present, of course.' From where the Jacksons were sitting there was no sign of any saddle of lamb. Instead, all they saw were twelve cubes of sheep-meat, carefully dissected from the bone and garnished with alternating sprigs of parsley. These Hassan solemnly proceeded to serve, one for each of them in turn like a prison ration. The very next morning Hassan moved on to newly-wed friends of the Jacksons, who had omitted to check his references.

Sir Geoffrey continued: 'His statuesque pillar-of-salt entrance at their own first dinner-party, to which we were invited, accordingly caught us unawares. So, too, did his flaming Christmas pudding, likewise promenaded on a lordly dish. It was blazing merrily enough, but somehow not quite with the traditional blue flicker. With it filtered from the kitchen the familiar Near Eastern whiff of the then standard Valor-Perfection range, ever more strongly; and, with the first spoonful, our young hostess looked round the table with stricken eyes. Hassan had this time forgotten to heat the ladle, and so had encouraged the recalcitrant brandy with a booster of paraffin. Hence the bright-orange flare-off at his ceremonial entrance. So yet again Hassan went on his way.'

Sir Geoffrey claims that in all his diplomatic career he and his wife only ever had three first-class butlers; and even then one turned out to be a voodoo priest; the other two were wanted for murder. Of the latter, the better by far was supplied to them by the Papal Nuncio. 'We should have remembered that the clergy always specialize in brands from the burning, nuns even more so. Yet Aldo was a faultless butler-valet, and totally honest with us – though he did wangle cigarettes out of the French ambassador, as a quite authentic ex-Légionnaire.'

It was the elderly Italian ambassador who subsequently told Sir Geoffrey Aldo's true past history. When serving with the Bersaglieri he had volunteered for the Russian front. Surviving as a hunted war criminal, he had then joined the French Foreign Legion, 'after graduating from which he had picked up more murder charges,' Jackson continued. 'The fact that Aldo had volunteered, for his own enjoyment, to inscribe all our invitations, menus and place-cards in an exquisite copperplate was explained by further outstanding warrants for his arrest as a counterfeiter.'

Aldo was the perfect manservant, however, devoted to the Jacksons according to his own code, and only really left them out of shame. 'At the Queen's birthday party, he had ended the evening in a hammock-couch, yarning and drinking our champagne with – and being poached by – the Ecuadorean ambassador,' Sir Geoffrey recalled. At midnight, Aldo and the other slipped away, abandoning the Jacksons to the task of trying to cope with the debris left behind by 150 guests.

'Before breakfast on the morning after, nevertheless, Aldo had already walked out on his new job. Feeling disloyal and too mortified to stay or return to us, he moved on – to establish a salami factory in the neighbouring Republic, which greatly prospered until, as we were so notified officially, there wasn't a stray dog left in the streets of the capital. Our last news of Aldo was a most affectionate greeting transmitted via Panama.'

Sir Geoffrey comments that the only real English butler they had totally lacked both Aldo's skills and his charm. 'Like Hassan, he, too, had Christmas-pudding trouble. This time it was flaming the classic pale blue as he made a ceremonial entrance with it into our Yuletide dining room. The snag was that there weren't any plates waiting for it on the festive board.' Being in a state of inebriation, he was unable to cope with this situation; instead, 'he halted abruptly, swayed, emitted a tremendous burp, about-turned and retreated to his bed – and, shortly after, from our lives'.

According to Sir Geoffrey, the English butler abroad in those days seldom corresponded to the Jeeves stereotype. The famous case of a previous ambassador's English butler and some French claret, also in Cairo, was related to the Jacksons by many an alleged witness. He recalled: 'I myself can certainly vouch that in those days there was a period every year when the mains water, filtered from the Nile, betrayed its riverine origin – harmlessly enough, but unmistakably. During the algae season, our drinking water was perfectly safe; yet no filter in the world could remove the essential oil, or whatever it was that left the tap water with its lingering flavour of algae.'

One night, on a particularly ceremonious occasion, the butler served some claret, which, after one sip, caused those present to exchange glances and covert smiles, for there was no doubt that 'His [notoriously thrifty] Excellency's claret carried an unmistakable bouquet of algae.'

For a long while afterwards people were to speculate as to whether the pro-consular claret had been 'watered with or without authority'.

*   *   *   *   *

Even the best of butlers can have their weaknesses. Mrs Astley Cooper had one whose adventures as a below-stairs Don Juan gave her such concern that she sent for him.

'Fred,' she began, 'do you know your Bible?'

'Yes, ma'am.'

'And do you know the parable that says you can't serve two masters?'

'Yes, ma'am.'

The old lady looked sternly at him. 'Then how on earth, Fred, do you suppose you can serve *three* mistresses?'

Pink sauce

Violent death has at times come as an unwelcome guest to a
dinner party. Cecil Roberts in *The Pleasant Years* recalls
how Norman Birkett told him the strange story of Mr Justice
McCardie, known as 'the bachelor judge', whom he once
visited at his urgent request in his flat in Queen Anne's
Mansions, near St James's Park. McCardie confided that due
to heavy losses playing the stock market he was threatened
with insolvency, which would ruin his legal career. Could
Birkett lend him £2,000? The visitor was then a practising
KC and his immediate reaction was that should he ever have
to plead a case before the judge and someone found out
about the loan, it could have damaging consequences.
However, as McCardie seemed on the verge of a nervous
breakdown, Birkett agreed to lend him the money providing
this was done in the presence of a KC who was a mutual
friend. But, despite Birkett's help, the judge despaired of
finding a permanent solution to his problems and took his
life with a shotgun. Subsequently, it emerged that McCardie
had been having secret affairs with women and was being
blackmailed.

Later, when living in Rome, Cecil Roberts happened to say
to Chance Quarrell, a retired solicitor friend, that he was
sorry to hear that Queen Anne's Mansions were being
demolished, and the other recalled how he had had an
extraordinary experience while dining with friends in their
flat there. A white sauce was to have been served with the
mutton, but instead it was pink. The cook, when asked the
reason for this, became very upset and admitted to her
employer: 'I put the sauceboat on the sideboard just before
sending it in and couldn't think why it was pink. Afterwards, I noticed there was what looked like a splash of red
ink on the sideboard. Look, ma'am, it's still dripping from
the ceiling!'

It wasn't ink, however, but blood, which had flowed
through from the flat above where Mr Justice McCardie lay
dying.

The perfect footman

The pride of the Newport establishment of the American hostess Mrs Nancy Leeds was William, her young English footman. He was over six foot in height, strikingly good-looking, with perfect manners, and his waiting at table was faultless. Then, shortly after the outbreak of the Second World War, he told her that it was his duty as a patriot to return home and join the army. She did all she could to persuade him to stay, pointing out that he was an only son and the sole support of his mother, but he insisted that love of his country transcended all other love, and stressed his firm conviction that God would provide for mother. Mrs Leeds rapturously described to her friends the noble intensity of feeling that lit up his eyes when he spoke of England. Promising to re-employ him when hostilities ended, she persuaded him to accept a gift of the equivalent of two years' wages as a nest-egg for his dear mother. She also bought a strong trunk for him and packed it with blankets, thick underwear, woollen socks and scarves, vitamins, toiletries and everything else she imagined would be of use to a rookie. Her generosity was catching; staff and friends showered the gallant footman with farewell offerings.

Before this prodigy left, he requested a small favour of Mrs Leeds – a reference. Surprised, she asked of what use that would be to him as a soldier. He explained that he wanted it for his mother, so that should he die on active service she would receive comfort from the knowledge that so distinguished a lady as Mrs Leeds held him in high esteem.

Some months later, Mrs Leeds happened to be a guest at a dinner party in California when she noticed that there seemed to be something familiar about the handsome young footman who had just entered the room. Sure enough, it was William.

*　　*　　*　　*　　*

Sir George Leveson Gower, at one time Comptroller of the Royal Household, knew a young footman who not only fought in the 1914–18 war but also won the VC for gallant conduct in it. He was rather overcome by the prospect of being invested by George V at Buckingham Palace and asked his employer, a young and attractive widow, if she would provide him with some moral support by accompanying him there. She agreed. When they arrived an official asked him if she were his wife or his sister.

'Neither,' he replied.

'What relation is she then?' the other enquired. To the consternation of both the young widow and the palace official, he answered with the damning, though true, statement, 'She is my mistress.'

*　　*　　*　　*　　*

Domineering, handsome Louise, Duchess of Manchester, who came to be known as the 'Double Duchess', had for forty years sustained a liaison with Lord Hartington. Then, following her husband's death in 1892, she married her lover who had succeeded his father as Duke of Devonshire. Whilst Duchess of Manchester, she employed a tall footman who resembled a good-looking mulatto and who treated her rather as John Brown did Queen Victoria. Owing to his autocratic and often outrageous behaviour she regularly used to dismiss him and then, shortly afterwards, treat him as if nothing had upset her.

*　　*　　*　　*　　*

Frederick Gorst in his reminiscences *Of Carriages and Kings* relates how, when he himself was working as a footman for the Duke of Portland, the Duchess came on a visit to Welbeck Abbey accompanied by her personal maid and a footman whom she called 'Black Jack'. With her she brought her own mattress, linen, tea and brown bread made of whole wheat-kernels. She proved very fussy about everything and especially about having hot plates at dinner, when Black Jack would wait on her. One night, she complained angrily that the one he had just given her was cold. Gorst says that the fellow marched in a fury into the serving-pantry and declared: 'I'll make it hot for her. This is going to be the *hottest* plate there ever was all right!'

Black Jack plunged the silver plate in boiling water until it was scalding hot, then, protecting his fingers with a thick pad, he carried the plate into the dining-room and set it before the Duchess, who burnt the tips of her fingers when she touched it: 'This plate is too hot,' she screamed, 'and you are dismissed!'

Unperturbed, the impudent footman replied, raising his voice: 'I will leave immediately, but I will leave with the satisfaction that your Grace has really had a *hot* plate at last.'

But Black Jack did not leave, and by the next day the Duchess appeared to have forgotten all about the episode. He was very popular with the Duke of Portland's own staff and, a week or so later, they held a party for him at the Worksop Inn. Unfortunately, he drank too much and behaved disgracefully, but Gorst and a fellow footman succeeded in smuggling him back into the house and putting him to bed. By next morning he had recovered, but someone betrayed him to the Duchess, who sent for him and asked whether the report regarding his shameful conduct at the inn were true. He admitted his guilt and she demanded: 'Why must you behave in such an indelicate manner?'

'Your Grace,' Black Jack replied, 'if I wasn't drunk most of the time I don't think I could stand being your footman.'

The Duchess froze and snapped: 'You may consider yourself dismissed and you will leave immediately.'

Gorst writes that Black Jack went to his room and began to pack his belongings, which was his usual reaction to these exigencies, but this time he did so as if in earnest, and they all assumed that this indeed was the final parting.

Then, twenty minutes later, Gorst answered the Blue Library bell and found the Duchess of Manchester seated at the writing-desk and holding an envelope.

'Gorst,' she said blithely, 'would you please find Black Jack, my footman, and tell him that I would like him to post an important letter for me in Worksop immediately?'

'Yes, your Grace, I will deliver your message to your footman as quickly as possible,' Gorst replied, hardly able to contain his laughter.

Shopping à la française

Employing foreign servants can cause problems when they go shopping. Before marrying the Duke of Bedford, the Duchess came to England to set up a television series and rented a vicarage where she installed her children and her Parisian cook Geneviève, who knew no English. Sent to the butcher to buy pigs' trotters, Geneviève tried to make him understand in dumb show what she wanted by pointing at her own feet. He nodded and jotted something down on a scrap of paper and handed it to her. Assuming from this that pigs' trotters in England were sold in a special shop, she went to the address written on the paper, which turned out to be that of a chiropodist.

Next, the future Duchess asked Geneviève to prepare a ragoût of pork, duck and white haricot beans, but found what was served at table uneatable. On being questioned, the cook admitted that, unable to find any beans similar to those used in France, she had bought a packet with a picture on the outside that appealed to her. They were sunflower seeds.

The French are normally far better shoppers than the Anglo-Saxons. The Provençal wife of an Englishman went to the butcher's to buy a chicken. There was only one in the window, priced £2.35. 'Have you a bigger one – but not more than £3?' she asked. The man had no more but was not going to admit it.

'Certainly, madam,' he answered, smiling. Surreptitiously taking the rejected chicken with him to the back of the shop, he stretched the skin as much as he could, wrapped up the giblets in plenty of paper and stuffed the bird with them so that it looked as if it had a wonderfully plump breast. Returning to the customer, he told her: 'There's something extra special. £2.95 to you, madam.'

'Merci beaucoup!' she thanked him. 'And I'll have that other chicken as well!'

Thirteen at table

To the superstitious, eating can be like living on the edge of a precipice. A misplaced crossed knife and fork can mean that you will be crossed in love – or worse. Always crush the shell of an egg after eating the contents or rap it three times and then stab it. If you do not, you may rue it before the year is out. Don't place your roll upside down, for that is the equivalent of cutting the cards and turning up the ominous Ace of Spades.

Before ordering cabbage, consult your diary to make sure it is not St Stephen's Day – the first Christian martyr hid in a field of cabbages, but was captured and met a tragic end. Consider carefully all the pros and cons before you drink the last drop of wine in the bottle. If you finish it, you may have to wed within the year or, if you are already married, there is a divorce on the way.

And, of course, never have thirteen to a dinner party. If this should ever happen, try warding off the bad luck by drawing lots and making the loser leap over your left shoulder and out of the house!

Thirteen at table

Those who scoff at superstitions may tell you that thirteen at table is only to be dreaded when there is only enough for twelve – and an overturned salt cellar only when it is overturned into a good dish.

* * * * *

Possibly the safest restaurant in London for the superstitious is the Savoy. It has six private dining-rooms, all named after Gilbert and Sullivan operas. The largest, the *Pinafore*, is the home of a 3-foot-tall ebony cat that normally sits on a shelf mounted high on a wall with a handsome mirror behind it. Should a party of fourteen be reduced at the last moment to thirteen, this lucky cat is placed on a cushion in the chair that should have been occupied by the absent guest.

The cat is carefully guarded because in the past it has been kidnapped – once by a pilot who flew with it to Africa. Before being recovered, it lost an ear and had its tail broken. (The damage is not noticeable, thanks to skilful repair.)

* * * * *

The songwriter Cole Porter, incurably superstitious, once invited fourteen to his home for lunch but was worried in case a last-minute 'can't come' message from a suddenly indisposed guest might bring about bad luck. Frantically, he phoned the others and one obliged by bringing along a young publisher's editor. Unfortunately, this Westerner broke all the rules of polite society that Cole regarded as sacrosanct. Afterwards he complained to the man who had brought him that the fellow had ruined the luncheon by trying to bring his cocktail to the table and not being able to speak French.

'He simply will not do,' Porter pontificated, then added: 'Besides, he wore brown shoes.'

What the eye doesn't see

Odd things can happen underneath the table. Charles Chenevix Trench was Anglican Archbishop of Dublin and Primate of Ireland for a decade in Queen Victoria's reign. During a dinner, he suddenly turned to his wife and exclaimed in a deep, doom-stricken voice: 'It's come at last! It's come at last!'

Horrified, she asked: 'What has come?'

'Paralysis!' he groaned.

'Paralysis!' she repeated, aghast. 'What makes you say that?'

'I'm certain of it. I have been pinching my leg at the very least thirty times, and I can feel nothing.'

'I beg your Grace's pardon,' broke in the lady who sat on his other side, 'but you have been pinching mine!'

*   *   *   *   *

Lady Diana Cooper recalls that at a dinner in London held in honour of Charlie Chaplin she was seated next to one of Britain's most eminent literary figures, who pinched her leg black and blue and demanded a kiss. Worse was to come. 'He seized my hand as the Commendatore seized Don Giovanni's and started to drag it to you know where. I was purple in the face not so much with the shame as with the strain of writhing away.'

Under the table is also a good place for ladies to shed their uncomfortable footwear. A mischievous small boy once hid under the table during a dinner party and mixed up the discarded shoes, then enjoyed himself watching battleships trying to squeeze themselves into canoes. 'If I'd found any butter, I'd have spread it on them,' he sniggered when caught.

*   *   *   *   *

Ivor Spencer in *Pray Silence*, diverting reminiscences of his career as a toastmaster, reveals how Princess Margaret once kicked off her shoes under the table. When a waiter unknowingly knocked into them the contents of an uncorked bottle of wine he had deposited on the floor an embarrassing situation threatened. However, Mr Spencer with admirable presence of mind and the deftness of a conjuror removed the shoes, dried and returned them before the Princess was aware of it.

On another occasion, Mr Spencer relates, a British cabinet minister using his new false teeth for the first time at a dinner bit too deeply into a lamb chop with the result that they became irremovably fixed in it. So, covering his mouth with a napkin, he slipped both into it and put the package by his feet with the intention of putting things right later in the privacy of the cloakroom. Unfortunately, when he looked later, it had vanished, having been swept away by a waiter and thrown into the soiled linen container in the kitchen.

'Mr Spencer, what have you done with my false teeth?' asked the minister in horror. To find them seemed a hopeless task but with the hotel's reputation at stake all available staff were enlisted in the search and the dentures at last restored intact to their owner.

*　　*　　*　　*　　*

Governor George Romney relates how a somewhat similar contretemps occurred at a banquet in the United States when the guest of honour cracked his upper dentures on a bone. He beckoned to the toastmaster and whispered what had happened, adding: 'You'll have to think up some excuse. I can't possibly speak.' The other gave him a soothing smile and passed him something under cover of the table, saying: 'Don't worry, sir. Here's a spare plate I keep in my pocket.'

The guest of honour changed dentures, then shook his head. 'No use,' he muttered. 'Too small.'

'Then try these, sir,' responded the toastmaster taking out a second plate, which proved too large. 'It's useless,' the man moaned, but to his astonishment yet a third plate was handed to him and this proved a perfect fit.

The speaker excelled himself and was rewarded with an ovation. Afterwards, he thanked the toastmaster warmly, declaring: 'What a bit of luck that you're also a dentist!'

'Afraid I'm not, sir,' came the reply. 'I'm an undertaker.'

*　　*　　*　　*　　*

Great Dining Disasters

The worst thing that can happen to a speaker is to find that all his notes have vanished. This was the situation in which Harold Wilson found himself when as Prime Minister he was about to address the company at a banquet. He had placed his papers on the carpet just under the table and the toastmaster, Ivor Spencer, recalling what had happened when a cabinet minister had concealed his false teeth there, decided it was best not to take chances so he discreetly transferred the sheaf to a small table behind him. Unhappily, Spencer had not realized that this was being used by the waiters as one of a number where they deposited large platters before serving the guests.

When they neared the coffee stage, Spencer went to put back the notes where Mr Wilson had left them and found to his dismay that they had disappeared. A waiter had picked them up with some dishes he was taking out. Spencer, aware that he was to blame, rushed in near panic to the kitchens, where all the bins into which the leftovers were thrown had to be searched. At last, the Prime Minister's papers were retrieved, but relief turned to horror when it was found that they were stained with gravy, among other substances, and were practically illegible.

Spencer writes in his reminiscences that the head waiter and he set to work with damp napkins and tissues employing 'an earnestness and delicacy worthy of the professors who unrolled the fragile Dead Sea Scrolls at Manchester University'. Despite this, the papers looked soiled and blotched but at least could be read, so Spencer hurried back and, unobserved by Sir Harold, laid them by his feet before taking up his position as toastmaster. Although it was clear from his expression that the Prime Minister was visibly startled at the state of his papers and glanced back at Spencer as though he suspected what had happened, he made no complaint and delivered a fluent and effective speech.

*　　*　　*　　*　　*

In the eighteenth and much of the nineteenth century, the gentlemen would wait for the ladies to leave the dining-room so that they could do some hard drinking. Round and round went the port and brandy decanters until one by one the guests would pass out and slide under the table. A

64

commodious chamber-pot would be circulated at floor-level so that no gentleman need disgrace himself by trying to totter to the lavatory and collapsing on the way. It was not unknown for a boy to be stationed under the table, too, entrusted with the duty of loosening the neckwear of the snoring sots.

When the drinking looked set to continue until dawn, servants would take the table apart, arrange a net in the centre into which empty bottles could be hurled, and stack the sideboard with additional supplies. Only then would they be dismissed for the evening.

*   *   *   *   *

In Victorian times such goings-on were no longer tolerated and the ladies expected the men to rejoin them after not too long an interval. On one occasion when the gentlemen were left alone their host, an English admiral, started entertaining the company with anecdotes about the habits of Arctic seals.

'When the bull seal feels amorous,' he alleged, 'he climbs

65

out of the sea on to an ice floe and gives a bellow that can be heard a hundred miles away. The females just can't resist it. This is how it sounds ...' The narrator gave a full-blooded bellow which sent everything on the polished table slithering and glasses somersaulting on to the carpet. Then the door flew open and the admiral's wife ran into the room cooing: 'Were you calling me, dear?'

*   *   *   *   *

Mrs Beeton in her book *Household Management*, published in 1861, wrote: 'Dr Johnson has a curious paragraph on the effects of a dinner on men. "Before dinner," he says, "men meet with great inequality of understanding; and those who are conscious of their inferiority have the modesty not to talk. When they have drunk wine, every man feels himself happy, and loses that modesty, and grows impudent and vociferous; but he is not improved, he is only not sensible of his defects." This is rather severe, but there may be truth in it.'

She continues:

> In former times, when the bottle circulated freely amongst the guests, it was necessary for the ladies to retire earlier than they do at present, for the gentlemen of the company soon became unfit to conduct themselves with the decorum which is essential in the presence of ladies. Thanks, however, to the improvements in modern society, and the high example shown to the nation by its most illustrious personages, temperance is ... a striking feature in the character of a gentleman. Delicacy of conduct towards the female has increased ... and thus, the very early withdrawing of the ladies from the dining-room is to be deprecated. A lull in the conversation will seasonably indicate the moment for the ladies' departure.

Mrs Beeton would have been shocked had she read Douglas Sutherland's *How To Be an English Gentleman*, published in 1973, and learned of the disasters now caused by the type's activities. He wrote that the final ritual for gentlemen before they joined the ladies was for the host 'to lead them outside to urinate in the garden'. Thereafter 'the resultant patches of dead grass on the lawn are put down to wireworm and the blighted roses are blamed on the damned greenfly'.

*   *   *   *   *

David Niven must have wished there had been a chamber-
pot under the polished mahogany table when he faced his
first regimental guest night in Malta as a young subaltern in
the Highland Light Infantry. As a newcomer he had the
doubtful honour of sitting on his taciturn Colonel's right. In
his delightful reminiscences, *The Moon's a Balloon*, Niven
relates how in the ante-room before dining the forty officers
and guests were served so many rounds of drinks that his
own bladder had reached bursting point when the meal was
announced and he found himself led into the other room.
His plight became worse as more liquids were served – a
cold soup and a different wine with every course. He could
not ask to be excused as 'officers and gentlemen never left
the table under any circumstance until the end of the meal
when the King's health had been drunk'.

Niven recalls that he sat in agonized silence with legs
crossed and with sweat breaking out all over him. When at
last the cheese was served, he was close to panic. He felt that
his career was about to end ignominiously. He saw himself
courtmartialed for causing a waterfall that would splash all
over his CO's trousers, soaking him to the skin and leaving a
vast lake on the mess floor. It was at this eleventh hour that
the civilian steward acting as butler came to him with a
message from Trubshawe, the eccentric brother officer who
had become Niven's closest friend.

Bending down, the steward whispered in Niven's ear:
'With Mr Trubshawe's compliments, sir, I have just placed
an empty magnum underneath your chair.'

The relief when he heard these words, Niven goes on, 'did
not flow over me – it spurted out of me'. Gripping the bottle
tightly with his knees, he directed the seemingly intermin-
able torrent into the opening with his right hand while his
left crumbled a biscuit. It was just as well that his hold was
secure for the Colonel startled him by speaking for the first
time. 'Pass the port,' he said, after inconsequentially mentioning his own all-embracing sexual prowess. He never
spoke to Niven again.

What the carver couldn't do

The host at a dinner party was very proud of his skill in carving and, having a surgeon as one of the guests, he could not resist saying, as he sliced the beef: 'What do you think of my carving? Do you agree with my wife that I am a loss to your profession?'

The surgeon smiled but made no comment until the carving was completed, then, pointing at the sliced meat, he challenged: 'You don't have to be qualified as a surgeon to do that. The tricky thing is to put it all back together as it was. Now let me see you do that.'

Skilled as surgeons are, there are some things most of them have not learnt to do. At a dinner held after a medical conference, a distinguished specialist sat down after making his speech and crashed to the floor as his chair collapsed under his fifteen-stone bulk. When it became clear that he was unhurt, a voice called out: 'Is there a carpenter in the house?'

*   *   *   *   *

Sydney Smith thought particularly highly of anyone who could remain calm despite a carving accident. Once when carving a partridge he splashed a lady guest with gravy from head to foot. He commented: 'Though I saw three distinct brown rills of animal juice trickling down her cheek she had the complaisance to swear that not a drop had reached her. Such circumstances are the triumphs of civilized life.'

*   *   *   *   *

In the 1950s coffee bars became very popular and a report in the *Journal of the American Medical Association* headed 'Espresso Wrist' read: 'Dr Kessel, an orthopedist, has described a wrist complication in those who operate the coffee dispensers. For each cup of coffee poured out, three to four strong movements of the wrist into full radial deviation have to be carried out, and in the average day several thousand such maneuvers are often made. Bartenders are not so affected, because beer is drawn with the wrist held stiffly, the elbow being flexed.'

This inspired S.J. Perelman to contribute an amusing piece to *The New Yorker* entitled 'Pulse Rapid, Respiration Lean, No Mustard', about a young doctor who, due to too many of his profession practising in his neighbourhood, cannot make ends meet. Then the first patient for days arrives. Lebkuchen, a tavern counterman, specializes in sandwiches and is suffering from a violent pain in the right knee, chiefly when on duty. Having examined him and found nothing irregular, Dr Binswanger declares he is suffering from a mild attack of corned-beef knee caused by the way he folds the rolls over the meat. In doing so, the patient is executing a half twist, throwing his torso's weight on to the right leg. The constant flexion of the knee, which pivots as he turns, is producing what is commonly known as cramp. To make quite sure that this diagnosis is correct, Dr Binswanger goes to watch the counterhand at work.

Yes, Lebkuchen is suffering from corned-beef knee, the medico later confirms, and he must not use that leg for nine weeks. 'I'd like to make a controlled experiment – study the malady under actual conditions, as it were. Perhaps if I were to substitute for you a day or two ...?'

Lebkuchen enthuses over the idea. To rest his feet just a few hours would be an enormous help – but what about the doctor's practice in the meantime?

'One's livelihood can wait, where science is concerned,' comes the noble reply, in the tradition of Pasteur. 'Maybe you'd have to give me some pointers on carving, though. To implement my surgical training.'

The other assured Binswanger that he could learn all within five minutes, and so it turned out. And by the time the lesson was over, Lebkuchen was declaring that the pain had vanished.

'Yes, that often happens,' the doctor agreed, but there was just one thing he wanted to know: in slicing the brisket did he go with or against the grain?

It was the salvation of Binswanger. An ecstatic, cured Lebkuchen recommended him to all his mates in the union. The waiting-room is constantly packed and the doctor boasts that he will soon be able to write not a mere paper for the *Journal of the American Medical Association*, but a book about the ailments he has discovered: pastrami elbow, caused by too much pressure anchoring the meat; skin pucker attributable to excess salt in pickle; salami foot, veal heel, etc., etc.

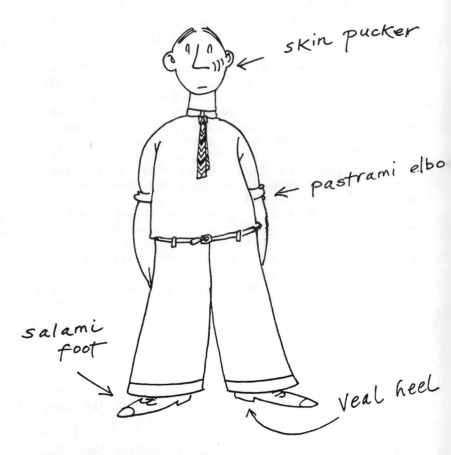

No dress for dessert

Publishers and Hollywood producers have found that there is a vast public for books and films about handsome young priests and nuns and their heroic struggles, usually in vain, to resist the appeal of the opposite sex. To overcome temptation and avoid disaster requires great strength of character. When still a cardinal, Pope John XXIII was Apostolic Nuncio in Paris, where he once found himself at a banquet seated next to a beautiful woman wearing an elegant gown which was provocatively low-cut. Instead of showing disapproval or agitation, he kept perfectly calm and then, when dessert was served, offered the enchantress an apple. She was puzzled until he said with a smile: 'Please take it, madame – it was only after Eve ate the apple that she became aware of how little she wore.'

Safer are the monks dining frugally with their brothers on an egg or two provided by their 'lay sisters'.

Etiquette outraged

Even nowadays, when almost anything goes, there are hosts and hostesses who will wince if you break rules of etiquette at the dinner-table and will not ask you back if your shortcomings are too numerous. The social climber anxious to find out what he did wrong might do well to study an appropriate manual.

Did he push past a bishop and a life peer, and in attempting to assist the lady on his left with her chair instead of the one on his right bump into the bishop who was doing the correct thing? And was he the first to remove the napkin from his cover instead of waiting for the hostess to give the lead? And did he tuck it round his neck to protect his clothes instead of laying it across his lap under the table? And did he wipe his lips instead of blotting them? Should he have pressed the napkin out on the table before carefully folding it up – like his former wife used to do with the sheets after they had had someone staying for only one night? No, he ought to have crumpled it and deposited it to the left of his cover.

That, unfortunately, was only the start of his *faux pas*. He had eaten holding his fork upwards in his right hand, instead of pointing it downwards in his left. He had laid his knife across the rim of his plate when not using it, had balanced peas on it, chewed with his mouth open, pushed food on to his fork with his fingers and then licked them.

Had he by the end of the meal stuffed his stomach full instead of leaving it one-third empty and not having to undo his buttons?

*   *   *   *   *

Even aristocrats of ancient lineage who have had the rules of etiquette beaten into them from birth can slip up on occasion. 'Harty-Tarty', the 8th Duke of Devonshire, dined one night at Windsor with Queen Victoria and the main dish was a superb saddle of 4-year-old mutton. As he was so talkative, she finished this course before he had eaten a mouthful. But it was the custom for the footmen to take away the others' plates at the same time as the monarch's. When the Duke stopped speaking for a moment and found all that delicious meat had disappeared, he was so upset that he snapped furiously at the footman: 'Here – bring that back!'

*   *   *   *   *

A more deliberate breach of etiquette was that committed by Lady Diana Cooper when in her youth she visited the Lord Lieutenant of Ireland at the vice-regal lodge in Dublin. On arrival, she was told by his wife, Lady Wimborne: 'I must warn you, dearest Diana, that in curtseying to His Excellency after dinner, we don't use the gavotte or Court curtsey, but rather the modern Spanish.'

Lady Diana says that she choked back the reply: 'You'll get what bob you can from me, plus hiccups if it's after dinner.'

*   *   *   *   *

Those who have reached the top, of course, are invited out to dinner and fêted by celebrity hunters whatever their table manners. But there can be a limit to indulgence. Laura, Duchess of Marlborough, knew Herbert Morrison well at the time of his being Home Secretary. She writes in her memoirs that when he stayed with her and the Duke at Blenheim, he never ceased smoking huge cigars and drinking lots of champagne. She did not regard him as attractive to women, but he was always trying to engage their interest and was immune to the cold shoulder. One night, dancing after dinner, he bit the Duchess's ear, removing an earring, which she told him he was welcome to, provided he either choked or spat it out.

The Duchess found one habit of his so irritating that during a semi-official dinner she felt obliged to protest, saying: 'Please stop scratching your head with your fork.' Perhaps, she comments, she should have admonished him in private – 'but either way it would have made no difference.'

Even those who are sticklers for etiquette do not always approve of its paraphernalia. Beau Brummell spurned finger glasses. When, at the end of a banquet, a flunkey brought one to him, he waved it away, then declared, as he stared at a man gargling with the water in his glass: 'No, thank you. I cleaned my teeth and washed my mouth before I came here.'

When the house is on fire

Arthur Balfour, the first Prime Minister to go to Buckingham Palace in a motor car, had also the reputation of being the most dined-out man in London. When Leader of the House of Commons, he ignored the rule that called for his presence there throughout a sitting. He would frequently slip away in the early evening and drift back hours later in tell-tale dress clothes, unrepentant and unaffected by any jibes.

Balfour's friend Harry Cust, who was described by Margot Asquith as 'the most brilliant young man that I have ever known' (apart from her stepson) and by Sir Charles Petrie as 'the most notorious lecher of the day', was holding a dinner party for twenty men, including Balfour, when the house caught fire upstairs. The talk, it seems, was so brilliant and totally engrossing that they took no notice. The meal continued while the footmen circulated bath towels with the port for protection against the water from the firemen's hoses.

Another example of typical British cool was displayed by a guest invited to dinner at a country house. Though taken aback to find the place ablaze, he did not show it.

'I say,' he asked his hostess, who was standing on the terrace encouraging the firemen, 'you did say this evening, didn't you?'

James Barrie entertains

What a red-letter day for a young novelist to be invited to lunch by a great author whose works he admires! Sir James Barrie was once editor of the *Nottingham Journal*, founded in 1710, and in 1923 Cecil Roberts, then its editor, wrote to ask him if he would send them a message to publish on the fortieth anniversary of his joining the paper. He did so and invited Roberts to call on him when in London.

In *The Bright Twenties*, Roberts relates that later he contacted Barrie, who replied that he would be happy to see him at 1.30 pm on a certain day at his flat overlooking the Thames in Robert Street, Adelphi. While making his way there, Cecil encountered John Drinkwater and boasted that he was lunching with Barrie.

'You're lunching with Barrie! What an ordeal!' the author of *Abraham Lincoln* commented. 'He won't say a word to you the whole time.'

Barrie's manservant showed Roberts into the large study. Drinkwater's prediction proved wrong and *Peter Pan's* creator talked easily, reminiscing about his life in Nottingham.

'But I was getting hungry, indeed I was rumbling internally,' says Roberts, for it was now past two o'clock. At last, as he was describing a visit to Max Beerbohm, the bullet-headed squat retainer entered and announced lunch, and the famished guest rose eagerly but his host signalled for him to sit down again, insisting: 'Do go on, finish your story.'

Roberts obeyed. 'At last Barrie stood up and led the way to lunch,' he writes. 'As we crossed the hall he picked up my coat, helped me into it and turned towards the lift which his manservant had summoned. He held out his hand. "Well, it's been a pleasure. I hope ye'll come again," he said. I entered the lift. He watched it descend. Down in the quiet dead-end street, I stood paralysed. Then my senses returned. "Lunch with Barrie! Lunch with Barrie!" I repeated. Holding on to a lamp-post I fell into uncontrollable laughter.'

Shortly following this disappointment, Cecil Roberts met Drinkwater again and related what had happened. The latter commented: 'I thought you were a little optimistic when you told me Barrie was giving you lunch,' and he went on to describe how one day coming across the playwright by the Savoy Hotel he had accompanied him to Robert Street. Barrie appeared to have something in his mouth and hardly spoke, but it was not food, for when the two men parted, he removed from his tongue a piece of wet paper and carefully peeled off a stamp which he tucked into his wallet.

'It's been nice seeing ye,' he told Drinkwater, making for the lift.

Lunching over the stables

The American millionaire Oliver Belmont had two passions – horses and the Gothic period. He and his wife also gave delightful luncheon parties at Belcourt, their impressive residence in Newport, Rhode Island, with its high pointed arches, lace-like ornamental carvings, and grand staircase – an exact copy of the celebrated one in the Musée de Cluny. The place was filled with an imposing assembly of antique furniture in the style Belmont so admired, but the most luxuriously comfortable parts were the stables with their steam heating and everything else he considered necessary for the well-being of his horses. The entire ground floor, in fact, was occupied by them and the eight expert grooms he had imported from England.

Belcourt became one of the sights of Newport and once a week charabanc-borne tourists arrived to hover inquisitively round the entrance taking photographs, while the more daring attempted to glimpse inside, much to the irritation of the owners. Soon after the Belmonts married, these unwelcome visitors arrived at the dessert stage of a luncheon party.

'Oh, here's that horrible man with the megaphone,' cried Mrs Belmont. 'He's going to tell those excursionists about our staircase. Just listen to what he says – it really is too funny for words!'

The guests stopped talking as bidden. But their hostess very soon regretted having made such a suggestion, for today the guide bellowed out an embarrassing new patter: 'Here before us you can feast your eyes on the new home of a lady you must have read about in the papers,' he told his flock, 'a society dame who has just been through the divorce courts. She used to dwell in marble halls with Mr Vanderbilt. Now she lives over the stables with Mr Belmont.'

At the captain's table

The captain of the *President Cleveland* once claimed that the worst experience he ever had on the Atlantic crossing was on the eastward journey when the ship ran into a violent gale. The ten important passengers whom he had invited to sit at his table staggered in for dinner already looking distinctly green in the face. He remembers greeting them thus:

> I hope all ten of you will enjoy being aboard. It is an honour and a pleasure for me to have – er – eight such charming people at this table, and to know that the – er – five of us will be dining together for the next few days. If any of the – er – two of you would like a rubber of bridge, I'll be glad to see you in my cabin. Waiter! I don't like dining on my own, so I'll do without the rest of my meal.

A popular and successful ocean liner captain needs to have a sense of humour. When the *Queen Mary* went back into service after the Second World War, special attention was lavished on first-class passengers in order that their word-of-mouth recommendations would attract business. They were urged in the dining-room to ask for anything they fancied, even if it did not appear on the outsize menu, and a prominent notice invited passengers on special diets to make their requirements known to the head waiter.

An American oil magnate ordered in advance rattlesnake steaks for four. The Captain was consulted and that evening for dinner the Texan and his party were served eels on a silver salver carried by two stewards shaking rattles.

*   *   *   *   *

Lord Shinwell tells a story about a girl who won the prize of a Mediterranean cruise in a Lincolnshire's Young Farmers' raffle. There was a condition attached – that she must keep a diary, true or fictional. Hers ran: 'First Day. Went on board ship. Second Day. Asked to sit at Captain's table. Third Day. Went on Bridge. Fourth Day. Captain makes improper suggestion. Fifth Day. Captain says that if I don't he'll sink the ship. Sixth Day. I save 866 lives.'

Dogs' dinners

For years, Harry Lehr kept New York high society amused with the diversions he devised. For example, at Mrs Stuyvesant Fish's party the guests had to dress up like dolls, converse in baby talk and be fed peanuts by a baby elephant wandering round the ballroom. One function, however, had unfortunate repercussions. This was the birthday dinner that 'King', as he was nicknamed, and his wife Elizabeth held for their dog, Mighty Atom. They invited over a hundred canines and their owners to the Lehrs' Newport home. There stewed liver and rice – in addition to a fricassée of bones and shredded dog-biscuit – awaited them on the verandah, set out on dining-table leaves laid on foot-high trestles. Soon not a scrap was left. A dachshund belonging to a Mrs Elisha Dyer devoured so much that it fell unconscious by its plate and did not recover until taken home.

A reporter who had gatecrashed was recognized and ejected together with his little dog. On the following day the front pages of the newspapers carried accounts of the event alleging that the dogs were fed chicken and *pâté de foie gras* served on silver plates. This caused a public outcry and the Lehrs and their friends were denounced for squandering money on animals when so many unemployed were starving.

A rival hostess priding herself on her svelte figure commented that she could never be seen with a fat dog for it would wreck her image, whilst another claimed she preferred hot-dogs because they fed those who bit them.

*   *   *   *   *

Joan Caulfield had invited ten friends to a cold luncheon at her home and the individual portions were all set out ready in the kitchen. Then, unfortunately, her cocker spaniel found its way into the room and ate one of these before it could be stopped. The culprit was put out in the garden and its mistress then took a little from each of the untouched nine plates to make up what was missing from the tenth. The guests duly arrived and finished the cold cuts. Then Mrs Caulfield happened to look out of the window and to her horror there on the terrace stretched out dead lay her pet. 'He's been poisoned!' she shrieked, and proceeded in a panic to tell her friends what had happened before their arrival.

Immediately the company heard her revelations, they decided to take no chances and all rushed off in their cars to the nearest hospitals where stomach pumps were at once put into operation to remove the suspect food. On returning home, Joan Caulfield was met by a neighbour. 'I am sorry about your spaniel,' she sympathized. 'I saw him run out on to the road and the truck go right over him. You were enjoying yourself with your guests and I didn't want to upset you just then so I just laid your poor darling on the terrace.'

*   *   *   *   *

Another American dog-lover believed that her pet should earn its special treats through exercise. Having taught the dog to beg for beef sausages, she trained it to run off with an order for some of the local butcher's own brand in its jaws. The man soon became so accustomed to such visits that he did not read what was written on the piece of paper his four-legged customer brought him. But when the creature began to appear daily instead of weekly, he became suspicious. On examining the paper he found it was completely blank. Whenever a longing for sausages had come over the clever canine, it had searched for a piece of paper and trotted off with it.

*   *   *   *   *

If food intended for humans is good enough for dogs with a palate, why should the reverse not be true? Certainly the TV commercials encourage such a view. After lunching with friends, a young man remembered that he had been asked by his parents to buy baby food for his sister and also something for the dog. So he stopped outside a small shop and asked the grocer if he sold small tins of the former.

'Sorry, I don't,' was the reply.

'Never mind,' said the youth. 'What about some tins of tasty dog's food?'

'Oh, you mustn't waste that on babies!' the proprietor

cried. 'There's a large chemist's catering for them just round the corner.'

*   *   *   *   *

Bob Guccione, the American casino, film and magazine tycoon, likes to cook Italian dishes and hold *Penthouse* editorial conferences in his New York home. (He designed its sumptuous interior himself and its fittings and furniture are mostly made of gold.) The meetings begin late and usually go on all night, as he himself never sleeps more than four hours, but his journalists find these marathons a strain. Once, it is said, such a meeting began in the early evening and went on without a break long after any of them usually dined. Then, to their delight, there wafted up to them from the kitchen a most appetizing smell of grilling steaks. How kind of the boss, they thought: he has read our thoughts and realizes that that's what we need to put new life into us.

The door opened and the butler entered bearing a platter loaded with enormous steaks, then he put one each on a number of plates and set them on the floor. In no time, Guccione's slavering ridgebacks ate the lot.

Pets at the table

Pet-lovers can ruin the enjoyment of their guests at dinner parties when they allow their animals to be present. On one occasion during the main course, the dog of the house kept jumping up, putting its paws on the male guest's leg and wagging its tail.

With a self-satisfied smile, the man told his hostess: 'You know, it's something I feel quite proud of – how dogs always love me.'

At this, her mischievous daughter told him: 'Don't be too sure about that. We're short of crockery and you're eating off his plate.'

*   *   *   *   *

Lady Diana Cooper loved chihuahuas and owned three in turn, all of which most of her friends thought singularly unattractive but which to her were heavenly creatures. Snug in her sleeve or concealed in a shawl, Doggie would accompany her everywhere. If she knew canines to be specifically barred that only encouraged her to breach the walls of injustice. Normally her favourite behaved well, but, if it failed to do so Diana would make all traces of the disaster vanish as expertly as any conjuror.

Once in a fashionable restaurant Doggie deserted its fond owner and left a large visiting-card on one of the shoes of a pompous director. So angry was he that Doggie just escaped being trodden on. Lady Diana, however, exerted all the magic of her charm and in a minute transformed the outraged man into a dog-lover who told the astonished head waiter that defecation brought good luck and that the presence of such pets made one feel at home in a restaurant.

*   *   *   *   *

Mrs Patrick Campbell was so fond of her pekingese, Moonbeam, that she never returned to England while it lived because she could not bear to let her treasure be isolated from her in quarantine. When she was in New York in 1938, David Herbert took them both out to dinner and afterwards back to their hotel in a taxi – the floor of which Moonbeam wetted, much to the driver's fury.

To pacify the man Mrs Pat, with all the art of a great actress, raised Moonbeam high before her, shook her finger at him and declaimed, like Hamlet after slaying Polonius, 'Who would have thought the old dog to have so much pee in him?'

*   *   *   *   *

Prudence Leith, the restaurateur, tells a story about a couple visiting the Far East on holiday. Finding that what they themselves were eating did not appeal to their pampered poodle, they called the waiter and to get over the language difficulty signalled that they wanted suitable food for the animal. The man nodded, picked it up and hurried off. Then, half-an-hour later, he came back bearing the roasted poodle on a platter.

*   *   *   *   *

The late Sir Ralph Richardson once bought in a Madrid market what he described as the finest parrot he ever saw. Later, over lunch at the Savile Club, he remarked that as José only understood Spanish he himself was taking lessons. Knowing how difficult Sir Ralph found the learning of foreign languages, a fellow member quipped that it would be cheaper to pay for the parrot to be taught English.

José was allowed to attend the Richardsons' dinner parties and on one occasion frightened Sir John Gielgud. When Lady Richardson went to his rescue, the bird bit her on the ankle. When Sir Ralph called it 'a brute' and 'a bastard', José swore back in Spanish.

The parrot was a lively addition to the Richardsons' household, but when it made a habit of clawing the chauffeur on the wrists the latter demanded as his price for not leaving that José have its wings clipped. This meant depriving the bird of exercise, so Sir Ralph would take his favourite with him when out walking.

Dining with duke and duchess

Meals taken together by husband and wife can sometimes be miserable even in the grandest surroundings. Consuelo Vanderbilt Balsan in *The Glitter and the Gold* relates how she dreaded dinner at Blenheim with the Duke of Marlborough when she was his Duchess: 'How ominous and weary they loomed at the end of a long day!'

They were served strictly according to the rules of etiquette: immediately a course was finished, the butler and his helpers would retire to the hall, the door would be shut, and they would not reappear until the Duke sounded the bell next to him. His Grace had a habit of heaping all the food on his plate together, then pushing it away from him, followed by the knives, forks, spoons and glasses. This he did with slow, deliberate movements. Next he would slide his chair away from the table, cross his legs and begin playing with his signet ring.

While thus engaged, Marlborough was deep in thought and his wife might not have been present for all the notice he took of her. 'After a quarter of an hour,' she wrote, 'he would suddenly return to earth or perhaps I should say to food and begin to eat very slowly, usually complaining that the food was cold! And how could it be otherwise?'

As a rule neither of them spoke a word. To calm her nerves, she took to knitting during these sessions, while the butler read detective novels in the hall.

*   *   *   *   *

Some stately homes are not only open to the public for visits but take paying guests. At Woburn Abbey one could stay for a weekend, the highlight of which would be to dine with the Duke and Duchess of Bedford in all the splendour of their dining-room, adorned with priceless paintings.

Once the Duke asked a guest what she thought of the Canalettos, and she replied that she loved them – 'especially with cheese'. An Egyptian stared spellbound in silence at the

same works of art for a while before exclaiming that he had
never seen better colour transparencies.

When the Bedfords arrived in New York on a long lecture
tour to publicize Woburn they were the guests of honour at a
dinner at which a man suggested to them that they could
help Nixon in his presidential campaign by telling people
everywhere how much they admired him. In *Nicole Nobody*,
her vividly entertaining reminiscences, the Duchess says she
replied that American politics did not concern them. The
stranger, however, persisted. The Duchess was wearing
mink. Wouldn't she like a sable coat as well? It was only
then that she realized she was being baited by one of Nixon's
henchmen.

At the same dinner party, a woman remarked to the
Duchess that she understood the Bedfords would be lecturing near her, and asked if they would like to stay the night at
her home. The offer was accepted, but on arrival they were
mot by the housekeeper who, explaining that her mistress
had a migraine, took them to their room and left requesting
that they be down by seven. To their amazement, they then
had to stand with the husband in a draught shaking hands
with some 250 business acquaintances of their hosts until
9.30 and without any refreshment. It was only when the
guests had departed that the Duke and Duchess were given a
whisky and soda. The migraine-sufferer had at last come
downstairs, but she soon complained that it was worse and
retired for the night. Her husband followed. So the Bedfords
were forced to go to bed without any dinner.

The Duchess writes amusingly about a similar experience
when she and the Duke allowed themselves to be badgered
into attending another party by a persuasive woman. By
10 pm no dinner had been served. They learnt that the staff
had gone on strike and that their hostess, who could not
cook, was in the kitchen attempting to produce a meal.

Hurrying to the desperate woman's assistance, the
Duchess, who is an excellent cook, fixed a towel round her
fine evening gown and made a fricassée, while the Duke
prepared a Woburn-style salad. And so another near-disaster
ended with some forty delighted people enjoying a splendid
dinner.

But there were more aggravations later during the lecture
tour. In Phoenix, the sponsor announced the Bedfords as 'the

Duke and Duchess of Windsor', while in Texas the long red carpet in an exclusive club was of such thick fur that as the guests walked up to be introduced the women's high heels stuck fast in the pile, causing several falls. The guests of honour could not help but be secretly amused by this until they discovered that they themselves had been standing too close to a fountain and that, as the Duchess puts it, her 'backside was dripping with water'.

In St Louis, the Bedfords were walking upstairs to the lecture-room after dinner when the Duchess overheard one of two elderly men ahead of them say to the other that what appealed to him most about talks with slides was that, being in the dark, one could happily go to sleep without anyone noticing.

Like the Duchess of Bedford, Lady Diana Cooper once had to wait ages for a dinner. She was in Moscow at the time, and when at 10 pm there was still no sign of it she strode, emboldened by vodka, into the kitchen, performed a Russian dance and sang songs Chaliapin had taught her half-a-century previously. Everyone in the place joined in.

'I was the whizz of the scullions,' she declares. 'They all kissed me, but I don't think the dishes were hastened.'

*   *   *   *   *

The 10th Duke of Bedford, who had a stinging wit, disapproved of his eldest son the Marquess of Tavistock's gormandizing, due to which he was very fat even from boyhood. Father expressed his feelings by parodying a verse of Isaac Watts' thus:

> How doth my little Tavistock
> His little self delight
> He shoots my pheasants all the day
> And eats them all the night.

When the youth left Balliol, his student friends entertained him to dinner because they thought that was the farewell gift he would enjoy most. The moment the clock struck nine, he became restive and soon rose to go. The others were astonished and urged him to stay.

'I'm afraid I must,' he insisted. 'You see, my landlady is giving me a special goodbye supper, and I happen to know

Dining with duke and duchess

that she has bought a huge Dover sole. I don't want to hurt her feelings by being late.'

On another occasion, when Tavistock was dining at Woburn, quails were being served from a large dish. His sharp eyes counted them and then the guests. There was one too few, which meant that if each person took one, none would be left by the time the footman came to him. Bedford's heir signalled urgently to the man to bring the platter over to him at once. Then, snatching a quail, he heaved a sigh of relief and fell upon the bird.

Banqueting with the Lord Mayor

Like most people, the Duke of Windsor did not enjoy listening to long, tedious, after-dinner speeches. In the early 1920s when, as Prince of Wales, he was present at a luncheon in Swansea in celebration of the completion of the new Town Hall, the Mayor droned on and on, oblivious of the growing restiveness of his audience. The Prince eventually whispered to Lord Birkenhead, who was seated beside him: 'Can't we dry this chap up?'

'F.E.' said, 'Leave it to me.'

Taking a menu card, he wrote something on the back and asked the Toastmaster to hand it to the Mayor. The message had a magical effect for almost immediately after reading it the bore ended his peroration. When the function was over, the grateful Prince enquired of Birkenhead: 'What did you write?'

The other smiled and said: 'I told him his fly buttons were undone.'

At another civic banquet, in more recent times, another mayor was warned in a whisper before he rose to speak that his flies were gaping open. He hastily pulled up his zip, but, on rising, swept everything on the table on to the floor because he had caught the cloth in it.

*   *   *   *   *

The irritation shown by the former Prince of Wales at having to listen to boring platitudes is understandable when one considers the number of banquets he had to attend. The press reported that at the Savoy on 12 January 1920 he shook hands with over five hundred people and was forced to change to his left hand halfway through the evening.

*   *   *   *   *

When the 6th Marquess of Londonderry became Viceroy of Ireland, he decided to cut drastically the length of official

88

banquets, by providing fewer dishes. Daisy Fingall says in her reminiscences that the average length of these dinners dwindled to half an hour, much to the disgust of gourmets attending them. A footman was stationed behind almost every chair and plates were frequently whipped away from guests before they had finished. 'If you stopped to talk, you would get nothing at all to eat,' she recalls.

One night Lady Fingall sat next to a Lord Mayor who was a slow eater, and while he was busy talking to her his half-full plate was removed and he was left staring in astonishment at the empty one put before him for the next course.

When he was offered cold ham, he gave vent to his feelings and told her: 'I don't call this a dinner at all. I call it a rush.' Then, disdainfully indicating the ham, he added: 'Cheap, too!'

Eating with royalty

Contrary to expectations, food at royal courts can be very disappointing. Take that of King Henry II, patron of scholars and poets in the twelfth century. According to contemporary accounts, the very bread – made in a hurry from the yeast in the ale-tub – was indigestible; to force oneself to swallow the sour and muddy wine one needed to shut one's eyes and clench one's teeth, 'wry-mouthed and shuddering and filtering the stuff rather than drinking'. So many people were invited that in order to feed them all sick beasts would be slaughtered and four-day-old fish served. The kitchen staff did not care if, as a result, guests became ill and perished, as long as a multitude of dishes were on view. 'Thus we who sit at table needs fill our bellies with carrion.'

*   *   *   *   *

Queen Catherine de Medici was an unashamed glutton. She once stuffed herself so full of the ragoût of cockscombs, kidneys and artichoke hearts she adored that she nearly exploded. Her son, Charles IX of France, almost suffered the same fate through over-indulging in *salemigowdis*, an Italian stew.

*   *   *   *   *

Cecil Beaton in *The Wandering Years* describes a weekend he spent at Wilsford as the guest of Lady Grey of Fallodon. There, over dinner, Steven Runciman related historical anecdotes of which the most bizarre was about Louis XIV's heart. It seemed that several years after the Sun King's death his heart was taken to England with much ceremony and reverence. This may possibly have been to escape the indignities of the French Revolution. Then, while being exhibited on a silver salver at some royal reception, it was mistaken for a little cake and eaten by a short-sighted clergyman.

*   *   *   *   *

Eating with royalty

The last Coronation in England to be held in Westminster Hall was that of King George IV in 1821. It was hoped that nothing would mar the brilliance of the occasion, such as occurred when his father George III was crowned. Then the Lord Steward, Lord Talbot, who led the procession which brought in the food, was horrified when his horse galloped in backwards all the way up to the monarch. This time the entry of the food passed without hitch, and well over three hundred silver platters piled with choice comestibles were successfully placed in position. But when the moment came for the Dean of the Chapel Royal to say grace he was found to be missing. When discovered at last he was out of breath and therefore could not be heard.

It was an oppressively hot day. The fierce sun blazing down through the high windows together with the heat generated by two thousand candles melted the make-up on elegant faces and turned them into gargoyles, whilst sweat ravaged coiffures and gowns. Through the negligence of the servants responsible, who were already drunk, the covers included only spoons, so fingers were forced into use and napkins became sodden with grease.

Irritated by the heat, the King abandoned the company and retired to rest. He looked like a travesty of a monarch with his belly let loose and, according to Lord Folkestone, now reaching to his knees. Taking advantage of his departure, some of the sightseers in the galleries made fishing-lines out of handkerchiefs which they hopefully lowered, while co-operative feasters tied chickens and bottles of wine on to them. This annoyed Lord Gwydor, already touchy having split his robe while helping the King into his. Lord Gwydor now started an argument with the Earl Marshal over their respective duties in keeping order, and, losing his temper, hit him with his staff of office. Pandemonium followed, and the great day ended with the King fearing revolution and having to be bled profusely.

*   *   *   *   *

King Louis XVIII, had he remained in exile and not ascended the French throne, could easily have earned his living as a first-class chef. Nothing pleased him more than to devise new dishes. His masterpiece was *truffes à la purée d'ortolans,* the recipe for which he kept a close secret from all in the royal kitchens and prepared himself assisted only by a trustworthy Duke. On one occasion, Louis's passion for his *plat* resulted in enough for half-a-dozen,.which the two men greedily ate.

In the early hours of the morning, the Duke was taken ill with the most excruciating indigestion, and a physician rushed to his bedside said he could do nothing to save the patient's life. Loyal to the last, the Duke sent an attendant to the King with urgent instructions to have him woken up and treated by all available antidotes lest he, too, perish.

'Dying? Dying from eating my *truffes à la purée!*' cried Louis. 'Why, I never felt better. I was right, then – I always said I had a stomach far superior to his.'

* * * * *

When Queen Victoria celebrated her Golden Jubilee, Queen Liliuokalani of the Hawaiian Islands was among those attending the festivities. One of the court officials has related how she insisted on spending the night at Windsor Castle where at dinner she told Queen Victoria: 'Your Majesty, I am a blood relative of yours.'

The latter looked astonished and asked: 'How is that?'

'My grandfather ate your Captain Cook,' was the reply.

* * * * *

King Edward VII and Queen Alexandra went out of their way to make their guests feel at ease. Gabriel Tschumi, the royal chef, describes in his memoirs an occasion when a distinguished Indian was entertained to dinner at Buckingham Palace. No special dishes of his country were prepared but there were alternative courses, one of which was asparagus, served plain to preserve its flavour and also with a butter sauce, the way the King preferred. The Indian VIP was tempted into tasting some. He found it delicious and when he reached the inedible ends of the stalks he began throwing them over his shoulder on to the carpet.

A footman narrowly avoided treading on a piece and gaped in dismay at the unconcerned Indian. The next bit nearly hit the hovering servant in the eye, but King Edward proved master of the situation. He, too, threw what he had not eaten over his shoulder. Within a short while, all the other diners were similarly misbehaving, and later when the cleaners arrived the usually pampered carpet was in a mess.

Tschumi says that there were a few grumbles from those who had to remove the stains, but when the story went the rounds of the servants' quarters there was nothing but admiration for the King's presence of mind.

*   *   *   *   *

The celebrated society gossip-writer known as Cholly Knickerbocker liked to boast of his connections with Mrs Simpson and in February 1935 he wrote in the *New York Journal American* that the Prince of Wales had taken up cooking in earnest:

> Only a few years ago we heard about the interest of the future King of England in needlepoint, and many remember how the Prince of Wales and Thelma, Lady Furness did marvellous chairbacks, stitch by stitch. Now, I am told, stitch by stitch has given way to stir by stir. All the latest cookbooks are ordered by His Royal Highness's equerries, and he has had a new gas range installed at his weekend place, Fort Belvedere, for his special use. Those who should know say he can do Chicken Maryland to perfection and the American hostess who is credited with giving him cooking lessons is none other than Mrs Ernest H. Simpson, the former Wallis Warfield of Baltimore.

Soon this story led to reports that the activities of the Prince's cooking coach had led to staff changes due to resentment over her interference in the Fort's kitchen and experimenting with recipes there. The following year another American journalist, Janet Flanner, wrote: 'In addition to being a good cook herself, she can make her own cook be a good cook.' Wallis believed that food had to look attractive. 'Leave it to the chef,' she said once, 'and you can be sure everything he cooks will be the same colour.'

When, as Mrs Simpson, she was living in a flat near Marble Arch, many a heated argument arose with fishmongers because she insisted that her purchases should be of the same size. Similarly-sized fish not only looked better when cooked and served, she maintained, but ensured that there was no risk of the platter reaching the guest at the end of the table with only the smallest trout left. Other retailers did not approve of the way she felt everything to see if it was tender, whilst the greengrocer was constantly grumbling at the sight of her punching and squeezing his vegetables and fruit as well as sampling grapes and peaches to find out if they were sweet. As for meat, the Duchess herself boasted that she knew all the cuts of beef; when the butcher failed to cut her the T-bone steak she wanted 'I produced for him my Fannie Farmer cookbook with a diagram showing how to cut a steak the way I liked.' She claimed to owe her strong constitution to drinking a tumblerful of juice squeezed from a pound of raw beefsteak every day by her mother – and also that she loved the taste.

*   *   *   *   *

One would not expect a Prime Minister's wife to drop a brick at a Buckingham Palace dinner party, but Margot Asquith had an unbridled tongue and no inhibitions. Indicating Queen Alexandra, who was talking to stout Lord Halsbury, she remarked to the man on her right: 'Just look at Beauty and the Beast.' Unfortunately, Lady Halsbury overheard this and she protested indignantly, refusing to accept Margot's apology, so the atmosphere was tense for the rest of the evening. Only the Queen, thanks to her deafness, behaved as though nothing untoward had happened.

*   *   *   *   *

Deafness was the cause of the stifled hilarity at another dinner party where a royal personage was present: in this case, it was Queen Mary. During the Second World War, when living at Badminton with her niece, the Duchess of Beaufort, she became sufficiently attached to a particularly well-behaved canine to reward it at the end of dinner in stately fashion with a biscuit. One evening she asked one of their dinner-guests, a bishop, to perform the rite for her, and handed him a dog-biscuit. Being somewhat deaf, he mistakenly concluded that she was bestowing upon him the Badminton equivalent of a sheep's eye at an Arabian

banquet. So, not wishing to give offence, he accepted the strange favour and gallantly munched at it until all was consumed. All present remained poker-faced and restrained their mirth until he had departed.

Deafness can lead to misunderstandings at any time. An old lady was seated alone in a railway compartment with a young man who was chewing gum. After a while, she smiled at him over her spectacles and said: 'You know, young man, I am rather deaf. I haven't heard a word you've been saying since you came in.'

* * * * *

Hearing aids can be a disadvantage to the deaf at social functions, where the amplified background babble obliterates the conversation of neighbours. Lady Wenlock, wife of a

Great Dining Disasters

Governor of Madras in the 1890s, owned an extraordinary ear-trumpet shaped like an entrée-dish, and once in Florence the attentive Italian aristocrat seated next to her filled it with an assortment of vegetables.

On another occasion, at a ball in England, she left it for a time on a piano. Later the Prince of Wales, who sat beside her at supper, started to speak into the trumpet but got a face full of cigarette ends and cigar butts due to male guests having mistaken the gadget for a fancy sort of ash-tray.

*   *   *   *   *

A *grande dame* of the theatre in Edwardian times always used the same opening gambit to her neighbours at dinner: 'You'll have to speak up, I'm afraid. I've become somewhat deaf. All that applause, you know.'

*   *   *   *   *

In 1958, Lady Diana Cooper was a guest at a Buckingham Palace dinner in celebration of a state visit of President de Gaulle, whose tall frame and bulky middle made him look like the Eiffel Tower about to give birth to at least twins. At dinner every time the service door behind her opened an Arctic blast lashed her.

'Can we do anything about the draught?' complained the French Ambassador on her left. 'My wife already has *la grippe.*'

'Can we do anything about the draught?' Lady Diana enquired of the Lord Chamberlain on her right, who repeated the request to a butler behind him who in turn passed on the plea to a minor lackey.

From the latter, the uncompromising 'Nothing at all' was conveyed back by word of mouth to Lady Diana, whose hair by now was blowing into the soup, which she, recalling the occasion, described as 'like nursery broth with bits in it'.

Saumon Balmoral républicain, according to the unhappy lady, were tasteless rissoles and the sweet, *glace croix de Lorraine*, consisting of 'a crucifix laid flat on a dish and dripping with cream and custard', shocked her.

Lady Diana found lunching at the White House no better, when she was entertained there in 1963 by Eunice Shriver, President Kennedy's sister. 'I loved Eunice,' she says, 'so I enjoyed the very inferior plate of dog's-dinner seafood poulticed over with tomato.'

Standards have at times been no better at London's No. 10 Downing Street. At a dinner there when Disraeli was Prime Minister, everything was served cold until at last the ices arrived melting. After contemplating them, the elegant Count D'Orsay leaned across the table and said to the future Lord Bessborough: 'John, at last we have something 'ot!'

The other tactfully pointed out that it could be dangerous to eat anything frozen for not so many years previously President Zachary Taylor had died through drinking too much iced milk with a basket of cherries.

* * * * *

In the Orient, royalty has often behaved with less inhibition than in the West. For example, Sylvia Brooke, Lord Esher's daughter, held a dinner party shortly after her marriage to the

last white Rajah of Sarawak. Conversation among the guests
proved difficult and there came a few minutes when silence
prevailed. Then, as she desperately tried to think of some
fresh topic, she heard a welcome sound.

'How wonderful!' she exclaimed. 'Just listen, it's started to
rain at last.' To her astonishment, the guests just stared
beyond her with varying expressions ranging from dismay to
ill-concealed amusement. She turned, and there was the old
Rajah heedlessly and happily peeing over the verandah.

Dining with the President

The most taciturn of American presidents was Calvin Coolidge, who once remarked: 'I found out early in life that you don't have to explain something you haven't said.'

This attitude put a brake on conversation at his dinner parties. On one occasion the lady next to him declared: 'Mr President, I made a bet today that I could get more than two words out of you this evening.'

Coolidge considered her for a minute, then he replied: 'You lose.'

Another time, Catherine Alice Longworth was his dinner-party neighbour. She was a brilliant conversationalist who prided herself on being able to animate anybody, no matter how reserved. But she failed with Coolidge, which so annoyed her that she told him: 'You must get terribly bored at all the dinners you attend.'

'Well,' he answered, 'a man must eat.'

Of the early Presidents, Thomas Jefferson was the most interested in gourmet dishes, perhaps as a result of his having lived in Paris from 1785 to 1789 as Treaty Commissioner to France. On returning home, he had a mould for making the macaroni of which he was so fond shipped out after him. When resident in the White House he employed two Frenchmen – Etienne Lemaire, his steward, who bought all the kitchen supplies, and Julien, his chef. This angered one politician, who denounced the President as 'a man unfaithful to his native victuals'.

Jefferson believed in putting his democractic principles into practice, but when he invited his butcher to dinner some thought he was going too far. To make matters worse, the man arrived with his son, saying that he had heard someone on the guest list had been taken ill. The President expressed pleasure at the butcher's initiative and introduced both to all the snobbish VIPs present, which they much resented.

Washington society was dismayed when Jefferson made it quite clear that he regarded all his guests as equal by having a circular dining table installed in the White House. He called it the 'pell-mell' system. One night the new British minister and his wife, Mr and Mrs Merry, came to meet Jefferson.

When dinner was announced, the widowed President offered his arm to his Secretary of State's wife, Mrs James Madison, while the latter's husband and the other Cabinet members did the same to the ladies nearest them, and the bewildered Merrys were left behind. The same thing happened at a dinner given by the Madisons soon afterwards.

This 'first come, first served' behaviour so sickened the protocol-bound British couple that they refused to dine again with either them or Jefferson.

In 1877, Rutherford B. Hayes became President and there was soon alarm among lovers of good living in Washington. Congressmen had long been addicted to liquor, hence the term 'a Congressional Nose'. Some forty years previously Colonel Davy Crockett, as a member of that body, had pointed out that under its rules they were allowed free lemonade, which they charged under the heading of 'stationery', so why should not whisky be thus allowed as 'fuel'?

His claim did not succeed.

Hayes and his wife disapproved of liquor and would not have any in the White House. This was regarded as a social calamity among the circles in Washington accustomed to being invited there, and the new First Lady was dubbed 'Lemonade Lucy'. A steward who secretly disapproved of prohibition found a way of circumventing it for the benefit of guests used to alcohol as an aid to conviviality. According to a contemporary account, the waiters were kept busy replenishing salvers of oranges within which was concealed 'a delicious frozen punch, a large ingredient of which was strong old Santa-Croix rum'. This, without Mrs Hayes' knowledge, would be served about halfway through each state dinner and was referred to by those in the secret as 'the life-saving station'.

It seems from his diary, however, that the President himself was aware of the reason why the oranges were so popular. He wrote that in reality only rum flavouring was added to them, to trick the 'drinking people'.

'Pray silence...'

Lord Butler once said that an after-dinner speaker should be like a lady's dress – long enough to cover the subject and short enough to be interesting. An authority expatiating on milk, for instance, could find to his surprise that some audiences prefer it condensed.

Choice of speaker is crucial: for example, a novelist might be a master of the written word, but perhaps not of the spoken. After lecturing to a luncheon club in the North of England, the author of a best-seller was asked by the programme secretary what they owed him for his travelling expenses.

'Nothing!' he replied loftily, having just received a large cheque for a film option.

'Thank you very much,' said the other. 'We are always delighted when speakers are kind enough to forgo their expenses, because the money we save enables us to afford better ones in the future.'

Of course, it is not always a speaker's fault that he fails to hold his audience. There may be distracting noises off. Once in the inter-city train on my way to an engagement I had a nightmare in which workmen returning from their mid-day break started attacking the road outside the window behind me with pneumatic drills just as I rose to speak. In my dream, the secretary went out and begged them to take a break, but their foreman would not have any idling at least not till 3.30 pm when they had a date at the betting-shop. I battled manfully to speak above the din. Then, normally meek and mild, I planned a diabolical revenge. It was students' rag week. I went into a phone-box, rang the police and bawled breathlessly: 'Students disguised as workmen are digging up the road outside the Queen Anne restaurant. Quick – quick – send a Panda to stop them!'

Next I went out and told the workmen: 'Students dressed as cops are on their way to shove you into a Black Maria they've hijacked!' And once round the corner I bolted for the train back to town.

*   *   *   *   *

Great Dining Disasters

There is a story often used by after-dinner speakers for an opening. A Roman Emperor was at the Colosseum, cheering the lions as they devoured Christians. Presently, he was amazed to see one of the Christians stand his ground when a beast approached him, and say something in a low voice which made the lion first hesitate, then retreat. As the Emperor looked on, the same thing kept recurring with other beasts, until, becoming exasperated, he ordered the Christian to be brought to him and promised to set him free providing he disclosed what he had said to the carnivores in order to scare them away.

The man replied: 'I just tell them, "I hope you realize that after you've dined, you'll have to make a speech."'

Pray silence ...

This tall story expresses the fear many people have of after-dinner speaking. Most of all they fear that their minds will suddenly go blank, forcing them to dry up. Some years ago, the mayor of a certain American town had to introduce at a civic banquet the celebrated airman Wiley Post.

'Fellow citizens, this is the proudest moment in my life,' he began. 'I am here to present to you a great aviator, who has just completed his astounding feat of circumnavigating the globe in solo flight. The feats of earlier explorers fade into insignificance beside the accomplishment of our guest, the great pilot, whose name is on everyone's lips. It is now my privilege to call upon the world-renowned ...'

Suddenly, an alarmed look came over the mayor's face as his memory failed him. He stopped and said in an audible whisper to Post: 'What is your name?'

Wiley in his reply said: 'Friends, as your mayor has intimated, I have travelled far but I must say that never have I visited such a fine city peopled by such beautiful women and capable men as in your world-renowned city of ...' The guest of honour allowed a dazed look to come over his face as he stopped and asked the mayor in an audible whisper: 'What's the name of this burg?'

*   *   *   *   *

Another mayor, this time introducing a celebrated couple from Woburn to the guests at a luncheon in Auckland, New Zealand, began: 'I am going to give you a few biological details about the Duke and Duchess of Bedford – I mean biographical.'

*   *   *   *   *

When Harry Truman was no longer President, he was guest of honour at a dinner in Des Moines. The coffee and liqueurs stage had just ended but the general conversation showed no signs of abating, so the chairman bent towards Truman and enquired: 'Shall we let them enjoy themselves a little longer – or shall we have your speech now?'

Many chairmen have borrowed these words since then. Lord Kilmuir in his opening remarks to the Guild of Cordwainers at their House of Commons dinner in

November 1954 confided that for the first time in his long experience the chairman had not turned to him and cracked this joke.

*   *   *   *   *

Impromptu toasts at a dinner can prove not only diverting but dangerous, depending on the *savoir-faire* of the speaker and the mood and constitution of the audience. At a diplomatic get-together toasts were proposed to the ladies of the East and those of the West. Then the new envoy seized the opportunity to make an impression and, rising, proposed: 'Now let us drink a toast to the two hemispheres of the ladies.'

*   *   *   *   *

Sir John Mills relates in his autobiography how, as the highlight of one of the Variety Club's annual conventions, a dinner in aid of children's charities was held in Puerto Rico at which Lord Louis Mountbatten was the guest of honour. On the previous afternoon there was a dress rehearsal of a commentary on his life, commissioned by Sir James Carreras and spoken by Sir John and Cary Grant at two microphones. These kept breaking down and the spotlights refused to function on cue, and to add to the confusion the hotel staff bustled to and fro noisily preparing the tables for the meal. Mills says that he can vividly recall Sir James, badly rattled and fearing a fiasco, muttering: 'And the trouble is, I hate bloody kids.'

Fortunately the actual performance that evening was a success, and was followed by a fine speech from Lord Louis, though even this had its fraught moments when a Marine guard of honour, standing at attention just behind him, fainted and fell with a thud on to the table. Completely unruffled and without a glance at the man, Mountbatten went on: 'You will notice that one of the admirable qualities the Marines possess is to be able to faint at attention.'

It was a typical example of Lord Louis's ability to cope with any crisis, and after the dinner had ended he further impressed those present by seeking out the unfortunate Marine to make sure he had recovered.

Pray silence ...

* * * * *

Celebrities noted for their wit could dine out every night of
the year and in return for entertaining the guests with their
sparkling speeches should at least be given an excellent
meal. After a dinner where the food served was so execrable
that he could not eat any of it, Lord Birkenhead took his
revenge. When asked for his address by the chairman, he
rose, said '48 Grosvenor Square' – and went home.

* * * * *

Great Dining Disasters

Disaster may threaten if the star speaker is believed not to be coming, then arrives unexpectedly after someone else has been roped in to take his place at the dinner. Robert Lowell was to have presented the prize to the winner of the literary award in memory of the late Lord Norwich, the former Duff Cooper, but unfortunately he suffered a nervous breakdown and was put into a mental home. A substitute was arranged. Then, at the last moment, when the guests were arriving, an urgent call came through warning that Lowell had decamped and could be expected shortly. The organizers were warned that it was vital, to avoid trouble, that he should not drink any alcohol.

John Julius Norwich rushed to the reception room only to find his mother, Lady Diana Cooper, chatting to Lowell, who was already drinking his third glass of champagne.

'Darling,' she said innocently, 'I've just been telling this gentleman how the principal speaker has lost his marbles and been carted off to a loony-bin.'

*   *   *   *   *

A popular writer of thrillers began: 'An author finds copy everywhere. Lunching here today has given me inspiration for an arresting opening: "It was nearly midnight before they scraped Uncle Harry off the dining-room table."'

Putting one's foot in it

Having to make an after-dinner speech in a foreign tongue can lead to embarrassment. The head of a United Kingdom trade delegation to Russia had a few hurried lessons in the language before going there. At an important banquet he attempted a short speech which he had with some difficulty prepared. Then, on rising, he hesitated, his mind suddenly a blank. He just could not remember the Russian for 'Ladies and Gentlemen' – and, being a Tory, he refused to call them 'Comrades'. To his relief, he noticed two doors in the far wall ahead of him. Those words painted in capitals on them were what he sought.

The speech, however, did not seem to go down too well. The atmosphere seemed as glacial indoors as it was without. A colleague had given a guffaw, hurriedly suppressed, so he asked him why. 'Because you began by calling them "Male and Female Urinals",' he explained.

'Soar' means in Hindustani a pig, and Mahommedans regard it as a term of high abuse. 'Sowar' is a trooper, 'billa' a medal and 'billi' a cat. Getting these words mixed up can cause unintentional insult.

After a dinner in celebration of Queen Victoria's being proclaimed Empress of India, the colonel of a regiment insisted on addressing the men in Hindustani, and this is what he said: 'Pigs! The Queen Empress has sent to me a number of cats, which I will now distribute among you. She orders you to hang them round your necks and to continue to wear them in that manner.'

*   *   *   *   *

An Eastern diplomat who had been Lord Lansdowne's guest at dinner caught him glancing at his watch, so he rose and said: 'My Lord, I must not cockcroach on your time any further.'

His host replied: 'Oh, must you go? Well, it's been delightful having the pleasure of your company here this evening.'

Then, when they were alone out in the hall, Lansdowne remarked: 'By the way, I should like to congratulate you on

107

the command of the English language that you have acquired during your short stay. I am sure your Excellency will not take it amiss, however, if I point out that the correct word is not "cockroach" but "encroach".'

'My Lord,' replied the ambassador, 'forgive me, but I was addressing you personally and therefore I used the word "cockcroach". Now, if I had been addressing her ladyship, your wife, I would then, of course, have employed the feminine form "hencroach".'

Another wife was unwittingly insulted when she attended a banquet in honour of her husband, Professor Hugh Troy, who, in recognition of his distinguished contributions to the field of Dairy Science, had been elected President of the New York State Dairymen's League. The Chairman in his introductory speech said: 'We are delighted to have as our new President a man who chose a cow as his life's companion.'

* * * * *

As regards ignorance of the English language, there is a well-known story of how the diplomat Dr Wellington Koo at a banquet in Washington sat next to a man who assumed he could only speak Chinese, and asked him in pidgin English: 'Likee fishee?' Dr Koo nodded and smiled enigmatically.

Then, later, after delivering a brilliant speech in Oxford English, he enquired on sitting down: 'Likee speechee?'

* * * * *

Even the most brilliant after-dinner speakers are often nervous beforehand, though they may have been doing it for years, and as a result only peck at their food. Clergymen with long practice are the least likely to be affected in this way. A young man, uneasy at the prospect of having to make his début, was told by the clergyman seated beside him not to worry.

'I can preach a sermon on any subject at a moment's notice,' he boasted. 'I just take off my glasses and talk as if there is nobody there.'

His neighbour on the other side took out a pocket dictionary. 'Suppose I open this at random – then stick a pin at random on a page?'

'Go ahead, my friend,' interrupted the parson. His challenger did so, then suppressing a snigger showed him the word. It was 'constipation'.

The pulpit prodigy, without any hesitation, responded. 'My text is taken from the Book of Exodus, Chapter 34,' he began. '"And Moses took the tablets and went up into the mountain."'

Another clergyman, asked to say grace, varied this to suit the menu. If he noticed the cutlery was limited to a knife, fork and spoon, his thanks would begin: 'For the least of these Thy mercies...' But a full place-setting would be greeted with an enthusiastic 'O most bountiful Giver...'

*   *   *   *   *

For those who are forced to frequent public dinners, the time they often wish they could creep away unnoticed is when the speeches begin. On one occasion after listening to a tedious talk by a politician, Dame Rebecca West whispered to Winston Churchill: 'Now I can say with perfect truth that you and I have slept together.'

When Sir Lionel Luckhoo was High Commissioner in London for Guyana and Barbados, he was supposed to be the chief speaker at a House of Commons dinner but the two politicians before him suffered from verbal diarrhoea. At last it was his turn and the toastmaster, acutely aware of the mood of the audience, announced with trepidation: 'Pray for the silence of His Excellency the High Commissioner ...' Loud laughter swamped his remaining words.

Sir Lionel rose to speak. 'Your Excellencies, ladies and gentlemen,' he commenced, 'your prayers are answered.'

And, to resounding cheers, he sat down again.

*   *   *   *   *

In *An Innkeeper's Diary*, John Fothergill relates how he made what some might consider to be a Freudian slip when at luncheon he offered four shy undergraduates from Oxford 'plum pudding or chapel harlot'.

Another entry describes how a friend of Fothergill's asked why all the undergraduates came to her tea-parties unshaven. He ventured to suggest that perhaps she had a peculiar effect on them so that they grew beards on the way. 'Yes,' piped up young Peter Quennell, 'a sort of capillary erection.'

* * * * *

Winifred Ashton, better known as Clemence Dane, the novelist and playwright, loved to entertain friends at her house in Covent Garden. She was celebrated for her *double-entendres*, which sounded outrageous but were uttered in all innocence, such as 'Olwen's got crabs' to guests arriving for dinner and, on another occasion: 'I've got a lovely cock'. Then, discussing the advantages of living in the country, she told Binkie Beaumont: 'Oh, the joy of waking up to see a row of tits outside your window!' Once someone she had given to read a chapter of the novel she was writing arrived early to lunch so as to explain to her before the others were present why she simply had to omit the sentence: 'He stretched out and grasped the other's gnarled, stumpy tool.'

Clemence Dane had a very carrying voice. The actress Joyce Carey relates how one evening after the two had dined they took a taxi to see a Shakespearean production at the Old Vic. On the way they discussed whether or not Bacon had assisted in the writing of any of the plays, and Winifred cried: 'Of course, Shakespeare sucked Bacon dry and Bacon didn't mind being sucked.' At which Joyce hastily closed the sliding glass panel between them and the driver.

Once when Winifred was staying with Noël Coward in Jamaica, after a lunch at which Binkie Beaumont, John Perry, Terence Rattigan and Cole Lesley were present, she startled the company by declaring that every man had five John Thomases.

Noël wickedly queried: 'Five?'

She went on: 'But it's well known, dear! There's the actual John Thomas he keeps to himself, and there's also the John Thomas of his imagination. Then there's the John Thomas he only allows his closest friends to see – and the John Thomas of his *other* friends' imagination. And, finally, there's the John Thomas he presents to the world in general!'

Being also a gifted sculptress, she used to hold modelling classes after lunch which everyone would attend in the hope of hearing more of her bloomers. Coward recalled her saying: 'Noël, dear boy, you must wipe your tool! You cannot work with a dirty tool.' After her pupils had covered the armature with clay she would command: 'Now then, stick it right up, ram it, ram it and work away, either from the back or the front, whichever comes easiest! Some people use a lubricant. I've used honey in my time! And remember, when you've finished you must withdraw it wig-gle wag-gle, wig-gle, wag-gle, ve-ry ve-ry gently.'

*   *   *   *   *

Dinners are often held in aid of some good cause. After one fund-raising function for a young people's hostel a speaker urged that the drinking of alcohol on its premises should be banned. To demonstrate its perils he showed the diners a live worm in a glass of water and another live worm in one containing whisky. Then, before the gathering broke up, he held up the glasses. The worm in the water was wriggling happily, but the one in the whisky was dead. 'Now, what is the moral to be gained from this?' he demanded.

A reply came from the back of the room: 'If you don't want to get worms, drink whisky.'

After-dinner entertainment

After-dinner entertainment in a strange land where the culture is entirely alien can prove a traumatic experience. Belle Livingstone, the much-married 'Belle of Bohemia' from Kansas, wrote in her reminiscences that she wished her tombstone to be inscribed with the words: 'This is the only stone I have left unturned.' Guided by such an outlook, it was inevitable that she should have experienced some alarming situations in her lifetime.

She was once the only woman among twenty Egyptians at a dinner party given by the Cairo millionaire Ibrahim Bey Cherif. After the feast, Cherif led Belle and his other guests on to the balcony overlooking the torch-lit courtyard to witness a second banquet. This time it was for a hundred naked dervishes, all gyrating and groaning as if demented. The Bey told her that they had been performing this rhythmic ritual for the past eight hours to demonstrate that human beings, through self-hypnosis, could transport themselves to a state surpassing both good and evil.

Once they had settled themselves to watch, a servant appeared below clasping a heavy basket. He put it down, cautiously removed the lid, and then ran off as fast as he could. Already innumerable small snakes were emerging and were streaking around the dancing dervishes, who, seizing those in their vicinity, bit off and devoured head after head.

'Wait!' Ibrahim Cherif told his stunned American guest. 'These are only the *hors d'oeuvres*. The next course is better!'

Servants were carrying in a fiercely hot brazier, bristling with sword handles, which they left in the centre of the holy men. The entranced dervishes drew the swords out of the fire and raised the burning bright blades to their faces. Belle blenched as the blades were thrust through cheeks, and almost collapsed as the smell of roasting flesh reached her nostrils. The Bey, noticing her revulsion, signalled to his underlings to take away the brazier and the swords.

'You do not care for the grilled meat?' Cherif asked her. 'Then I will toss them some vegetables.' At his bidding, a minion rushed over to some cactuses growing in a corner of the yard. With a sharp knife he sawed off a heap of spiked stalks and threw them into the air among the dervishes, who caught them and stuffed them, thorns and all, into their mouths, consuming them as though they were the greatest delicacies.

The Bey chortled. 'And now for a nice dessert, eh?' This consisted of thick glass tumblers: each holy man seized and crunched one with enjoyment, making a softly musical sound.

'Is there anything further you would suggest?' Belle's host asked solicitously.

'A glass of brandy for me,' she says was her reply. 'And I hope Allah appreciates all this.'

*   *   *   *   *

In Edwardian England dinner parties were often followed by musical recitals, but it was not unknown for guests of an amorous disposition to creep away from these in search of an unoccupied room. One hostess of the day, showing an innocent young girl the library, threw open the door to discover a couple making love in front of the fire. Tactfully, she murmured: 'Mending the hearth rug – how very kind.'

Escaping gas

The wise diner-out at important functions where he wishes to make a good impression should refrain from eating beans, cabbage and onions for at least twenty-four hours beforehand, and should be guided by the advice of American research scientists who have excluded these vegetables from the diets of astronauts in orbit on account of their 'flatus-producing effects'.

In polite society the freeing from confinement of digestive gases, whether audibly or not, is regarded as an odious offence. One cannot blame the Victorians for this as permissive Philistines might be inclined to do, for as far back as the 6th century BC such behaviour was taboo in China, while in India four hundred years later Kautilya forbade any man serving at Court to indulge 'in loud laughter when there is no joke, nor break wind'. In Imperial Rome, too, the practice was banned – though the Emperor Claudius considered allowing it when one of his entourage made himself quite ill by restraining himself.

In Baghdad, when a caliph proposed honouring Ibn Al Junayd by appointing him a boon companion, the post was refused because, declared Ibn, he felt more at ease mixing in humbler circles 'where one can pass gas in this or that direction without much fuss being made about it'.

Sir John Harington in *The Englishman's Doctor* published in 1608 included with approval a translation of a passage from the *Regimen* of Salerno, celebrated for his school of medicine:

> Great harms have grown and maladies exceeding
> By keeping in a little blast of wind:
> So cramps and dropsies, colics have their bleeding,
> And mazed brains, for want of vent behind.

Nowadays in our liberated society there is no need for such warnings. Indeed, in some quarters, farting has become fashionable fun. In 1947, Noël Coward and Graham Payn went to stay with the Lunts in their home at Genesee. Alfred was as superb a gourmet cook as he was an actor and they found every meal an unforgettable gastronomic feast. Noël with his small appetite feared he was going to burst, and

115

after a week wrote to Cole Lesley: 'Dinner tonight was the *coup de grâce* – shrimps *à la Créole*, corn peas, pimentoes, custard pie, tartlets and a series of explosions of wind that are still continuing as I write. Graham is blowing himself in and out of the room like a pop-gun.'

Graham informed Cole that Noël once broke wind so loudly that Lynn Fontanne called out 'Bravo!' from two or three rooms away.

Feasting on the film set

Eating under the glare of hot lights of a studio set can prove an ordeal, especially if the artists are supposed to be enjoying a birthday feast. In 1933 Josef von Sternberg shot *The Scarlet Empress* in Hollywood with Marlene Dietrich in the title role, and with Sam Jaffe as the Grand Duke Peter. Jaffe has descibed how Sternberg spent several days over filming a court banquet scene. Eventually, the most eye-catching 'prop' on the table, a boar's head situated in front of Marlene Dietrich, started to stink, a fierce spotlight having been trained on it for some time. The star endured the olfactory misery as long as she could, then fainted.

Sternberg behaved as though Dietrich were making a fuss over nothing and, when smelling salts had revived her, grumbled in German, 'Would I make you do this if it wasn't necessary? You must go on for the sake of the picture.' After he had agreed to do his best to find a fresh boar's head by the next day she resumed the role.

According to Jaffe Sternberg made Louise Dresser as the Dowager Empress go on and on blowing out the birthday candles 'as though she had a thousand birthdays to cele- brate'. When she flagged, he bawled, 'More breath! More breath!'

Eventually she had had enough and left the set crying, 'There ain't no more breath!' At last she returned, but insisted on one condition – 'No more candles'.

Jaffe also says that Sternberg in this banquet scene loved to ride over the table on a boom as if he were on horseback. On one occasion, he shouted, 'Everyone out! I want an empty stage!' All obeyed him save a small man in the corner. Jo roared, 'Didn't you hear what I said? I said, "Clear the stage!"'

'But, Mr Sternberg,' the offender pointed out, 'have you forgotten? I'm the cameraman.'

Richard Kollorsz, one of the designers for *The Scarlet Empress*, has related how when they ran the rough-cut of the film, Sternberg said very loudly at the end, 'This would be a great picture – if you took the actors and actresses out of it.' The epic proved a box-office disaster.

When bare bosoms shocked

For an elegant, exclusive restaurant priding itself on its observance of the proprieties any breach of its rules can be near-catastrophic. When rag-time became the rage in New York, the younger set began to fret against what they regarded as antediluvian restrictions in restaurants, but it needed some social leaders to start such a rebellion with any chance of success.

Mamie Fish and Fannie Burke-Roche were eager to launch new fashions and they had discovered that in London it was already regarded as respectable for women to wear low-cut evening gowns in the most exclusive places. Fannie Burke-Roche, who looked enchanting décolleté, told everybody in her circle that she considered it ridiculously prim and puritanical that men should be prevented from admiring those soft shapely slopes below a lady's neck except within the confines of private houses.

'We must broaden people's minds,' she told her close friend, Mamie, whom nature had endowed with physical charms similar to Fannie's, 'but we must begin gradually. Next Sunday evening at Sherry's we will go without hats. You can wear your dress with the bretelles, and I will wear mine with the Dutch neck.'

But their beaux were not so brave and one after the other made excuses for not accompanying them. At last, however, two fearless fellows were badgered into supporting them, and the quartet walked into Sherry's one evening when every table was occupied except theirs – deliberately reserved in a conspicuous position. The flunkeys taking charge of the ladies' stoles almost dropped them.

'Shocking!' 'Brazen!' 'Most offensive!' 'Depraved!' Such were the comments exclaimed by outraged diners. Louis Sherry himself shuddered but managed to control his feelings as he hastened towards the culprits with the intention of asking them to leave. However, on recognizing them, he changed his mind. They had caused a sensation, but it would cause an even greater one if he turned away society lionesses of their standing. So in silent resignation he ushered them to their table and beckoned to his head waiter.

By the end of the evening, Mamie and Fannie were aware that the storm of disapproval aroused by them on arrival had dispersed to a significant extent and some were now studying them with grudging enjoyment and envy. The innovators felt they had won, and the following Sunday proved it when a number of ladies came similarly exposed to that bastion of strict etiquette.

But the revolt did not stop there. Less than two years later, Louis Sherry one lunch-time was dismayed to see Mrs Edith Gould open a luxurious vanity-case she had acquired in Paris and, watched by the whole restaurant, ostentatiously powder her nose and coat her lips with a bright rouge. Almost running to her, he asked anxiously if she were feeling indisposed? Could he not conduct her to the *toilette pour les dames*? But she refused to take the hint and, replying that she was in the best of health, went on making up her face. Louis Sherry retreated, aware that yet another of his cherished conventions had been discarded.

Nevertheless, there were limits to the great restaurateur's tolerance. One Sunday evening, Mrs Frederick Havemeyer insolently lighted up while dining and started blowing smoke rings into the air. Courteously, he made it clear to her that she must either put the cigarette out or go. She yielded.

Where *Eve* dared not tread

Men's clubs have long resisted the admission of women, the old guard there considering that it would be intolerable to hear the sound of feminine chatter and laughter within their strongholds. Nevertheless, the daughters of Eve are gradually infiltrating them. One evening an old member came into his club of ancient vintage and was outraged to find not only women there, but one daring to lounge in his favourite armchair. He stumped into the secretary's office and demanded an explanation.

'The committee has decided to allow members to bring their wives in for dinner,' the other told him, 'so as to try and keep solvent.'

'But I'm a bachelor. Such discrimination is grossly unfair,' complained the member. 'Could I bring a girl friend?'

The secretary reflected for a moment, then he replied: 'I think it might be all right, provided she is the wife of a member.'

When another club decided to be more adventurous still and to admit women to full membership, a QC applied in a Chancery Court for the necessary permission to alter the wording in the founding document of the club. In a long speech, he pointed out the social changes that had occurred in the past hundred years and stressed the financial problems besetting the management. He painstakingly read out the proposed alterations, adding 'or she' to 'he' and so on.

The Judge gave his consent to all these amendments, then he remarked: 'There remains a phrase in the document before me which it would seem you wish to leave as it is, possibly because it might in time ensure the club's continuance. I refer to the opening sentence on page one, which reads: "The object of the club is to encourage intercourse between the members."'

Snubs for snobs

Grace Vanderbilt, wife of Cornelius the younger, prided herself on having succeeded Mrs Astor as the leader of New York society. When intending to dine at Ciro's in Monte Carlo, she was dissatisfied with the table reserved for her and sent for the *maître d'hôtel*. She indicated another table and asked to be moved there, but was told it was being kept for Prince Danilo of Montenegro. So she pointed at one in a corner, but that one had been bespoken by an English duchess.

'In that case,' snapped Mrs Vanderbilt, 'see that you give me a better table than the Duchess's in future.' She turned to an Englishman she knew sitting nearby and said loftily: 'It is only here in France that I am treated like this. In America, I take a rank something like that of your Princess of Wales.'

'Oh,' returned the Englishman, 'then who is your Queen?'

Grace was very proud of her friendship with the Royal Family. Later on, when the Princess of Wales had become Queen Mary, Sir Osbert Sitwell used to visit Grace's *'château'* on Fifth Avenue. Once, before returning to London, he asked if he could do anything for her on returning there, and she said: 'Only give my love to the dear boys.' He wrote in his memoirs that he knew at once whom she meant – the Prince of Wales, and the Dukes of York, Gloucester and Kent.

In England, when both were guests for dinner of Mrs Ronnie Greville at Polesden Lacey, Sir Osbert complimented Mrs Vanderbilt on the colour of her dress and he relates that 'in happy innocency' she answered: 'Yes, that is why in New York I am known as the Kingfisher.'

At that time, says Sitwell, she was 'one of the most conventional people alive', but with age she changed, as he discovered several years later when seated beside her at a large luncheon party in New York. She startled him by gesticulating in the direction of a much-publicized general on the opposite side of the table who was holding forth as if addressing a public meeting.

'That man is too noisy – I shall scream,' she declared.

And, before Sir Osbert could restrain her, Grace gave a yell 'loud and fierce enough to have done credit to an American

122

Indian out for a day's scalping'. Unperturbed by the sensation this caused, she asked Sitwell: 'Shall I scream again?' But he managed to soothe her. To the end, she never tired of mentioning her close friendship with royals, and when she met the Soviet Ambassador at a banquet she could not resist opening the conversation with the gambit: 'I was devoted to your Tzar.'

       *   *   *   *   *

In the Boston society of the old days, snobs would boast that an ancestor had come over with the *Mayflower*. Asked by her hostess at a dinner if her family had come over from England on the second boat, a Mrs Harrington Grey replied: 'We sent our servants ahead on the first to get things ready for us.' Mrs Jack Gardner, bored by a guest with similar pretensions, commented: 'Indeed. I understand the immigration laws are much stricter nowadays.'

       *   *   *   *   *

Lord Birkenhead silenced for the rest of the dinner a woman seated next to him who introduced herself as 'Mrs Porter-Porter with a hyphen', to which he quipped, 'And I'm Mr Whisky-Whisky with a syphon.'

Are outsized Eves dangerous?

Suppose you are very much in love with some enchantress who, when you take her out to dine, eats and eats and eats. Hold back – don't pop the question. Be advised by Dr Samuel Johnson, who wrote in a letter: 'If once you find a woman gluttonous, expect from her very little virtue.'

Sydney Smith, who was thirteen years old when Johnson died, held similar views. Somebody told him that a young Scot was going to marry an Irish widow twice his age and more than twice his size. 'Going to marry her? Impossible!' Smith wrote. He continued:

> You mean a part of her; he could not marry her all himself. It would be a case, not of bigamy, but trigamy; the neighbourhood or the magistrates should interfere. There is enough of her to furnish wives for a whole parish. One man marry her! It is monstrous! You might people a colony with her; or perhaps take your morning's walk round her, always provided there were frequent resting-places, and you were in rude health. I once was rash enough to try walking round her before breakfast, but only got half-way and gave it up exhausted. Or you might read the Riot Act and disperse her, in short, you might do anything with her but marry her.

Today's males might be prevented from making a similar mistake by not allowing such a woman to tempt them into eating artichokes. Not for nothing did street vendors used to cry in Paris, a city where the wiles of women are well understood: 'Artichokes! Artichokes! Heats the body and the spirit. Heats the genitals.'

*　　*　　*　　*　　*

The Perfumed Garden, that treasury of Arabic sexual practices originally penned in 1410 by Shaykh Nafzawi and translated from the French version in 1888 by Sir Richard Burton, contains several warnings as to what not to eat. Coitus after fish, we are cautioned, leads to insanity, after milk to paralysis, after camel-meat and lentils to varicose veins and gout, after aubergines to hot flushes. But those much-maligned onions, if boiled in jasmine oil, make the perfect ointment for turning breasts into ripe pomegranates.

Stealing and swopping

Leaving something precious on your car while you have a meal can prove a costly mistake. In *Ancestral Voices*, James Lees-Milne recalls a true story told to him by Morogh Bernard when dining at the Ritz. It concerned a Belgian friend who at the time of the Second World War went off in her car when the Nazis poured over the frontier. She was accompanied by her frail, wealthy aunt, who died during the journey. It was too risky to stop and have the old lady interred, so the niece left the body on the back seat and drove on.

But it was fiercely hot and on the fourth day the fugitive was forced to roll up the remains in some valuable rugs and rope them to the roof of the vehicle. Presently, she stopped at a café and went inside for something to eat. By the time she emerged again, thieves had removed the rugs and their contents. Neither was recovered and for the niece it was a double disaster, for as the death could not be legally certified she had to wait thirty years before she could inherit her aunt's money.

*   *   *   *   *

An Englishman once received something in exchange when there was a mix-up over his wife's remains following her demise through food poisoning in India, where as a journalist she had been on a fact-finding visit. He asked for her body to be embalmed and shipped back home, but when the coffin was opened it contained instead a general in full dress uniform. He immediately cabled the undertakers and their response read: 'Wife buried with full military honours. You may keep general.'

*   *   *   *   *

For many a gourmet passionately in love with the pleasures of the table, the loss of a rare recipe or food would transcend that of any kith and kin. That doyen of humorists, S.J. Perelman, was inspired to write 'Heat Yeggs in Vessel and Sprinkle with Hazard' by reading an advertisement in the

Stealing and swopping

New York Times describing how Macy's taster had spent his life searching the world for better, rarer, more exotic delicacies. Other sources of inspiration were a note on the menu of Mrs Toffenetti's restaurant that her Italian spaghetti was served with mushroom sauce made from a treasured old recipe discovered by her in the archives of an ancient castle in Bologna, and an article in the *Journal-American* which revealed that another restaurateur, Romeo Salta, thought nothing of having his breadsticks flown over daily from Italy, and his lemons from Cuba.

From these ingredients, Perelman concocted his own satire. In the buffet of the Gare Saint-Lazare, Norman Popenoe sits beside him, sniffs at the stains on his suit and correctly deduces that he has eaten lobster bisque at Prunier's, *foie gras* at the Périgourdine, and the wrong dish at Le Chien Qui Fume. This gastronomic Sherlock Holmes then reveals that he is the senior taster for a Milwaukee department store, whose job it is to buzz round the globe rooting out anything that contributes to gracious living, such as baby squid, sea urchins, stewed iguana, and fried locusts.

Great Dining Disasters

He has not eaten at home for forty-three years – no loss as his wife is the worst cook in Christendom.

The two men meet again on the ship *Dyspepsia* where they sit at Captain Lovibond's table together with two restaurateurs, Mrs Fettucini (whom Popenoe likens to the faded meringues one avoids in pastry shops), and portly Mr Balderdacci. Both have been combing Italy for gastronomic marvels to please their discerning patrons and are soon engaged in a verbal duel bragging about what they have acquired. She has unearthed a fantastic recipe for gnocchi in the ruins under the Marchesa di Rigmarole's castle and he has acquired six exquisite green peppers, all locked in their state rooms. Then a double disaster occurs, for these treasures are stolen.

Sherlock Popenoe gets Perelman's promise of co-operation in preparing a trap to catch the thief. 'At dinner tonight, I shall entrust to your safekeeping, with a tedious preface about its value, a canister of Irish oatmeal I discovered in Maynooth. Express misgivings, shun the responsibility, but acquiesce. Then take it to your cabin, put out the lights, and lie doggo till I arrive.' Popenoe warns him to take care, for he is sure that this gourmet crook will stop at nothing to get that porridge.

The plot succeeds. 'Captain Lovibond' is caught breaking in. Popenoe tears off his false red beard and tinted glasses to unmask Rory Pachyderm, taster for Springer, Uris & Bodkin's in Cleveland – 'the twisted genius behind every culinary snatch of our time, a Moriarty so devoid of conscience that he would heist a child's onion from its Martini or a cripple's anchovy paste if it served his ends.'

Popenoe's suspicions had been roused through Pachyderm's referring to the ship's funnels as chimneys and the hold as the basement that first night at dinner. As for the real Captain, he was found trussed up as neatly as a fowl in the chart-room closet where the villain had imprisoned him.

Childish behaviour

When Prince Arthur of Connaught was at Eton he wrote to his grandmother asking her for £5 so that he could buy extra food over Christmas at the college tuck-shop. Queen Victoria refused, advising him to curb his expensive tastes. He wrote back to her: 'Dear Granny, please don't bother at all about the £5, because I have sold your letter to another boy for £7.'

A contemporary of Prince Arthur's, Sir George Leveson Gower, relates in his reminiscences that when he was small his nurse used to read the Bible to him. Once 'Pagey' was not alert enough to skip a passage about committing fornication. The boy asked what this meant and, with commendable presence of mind, she replied that it was another way of telling one not to be dirty. A few days later, his father visited the nursery at tea-time. 'Pagey' had just spilt some jam, so, delighted at the opportunity of airing his newly acquired vocabulary, little George observed, to her confusion: 'Look, papa, Pagey has been committing fornication on the table-cloth.'

Sir George, Comptroller of the Royal Household from 1892 to 1895, was at Court when Queen Victoria asked a former maid-of-honour who had married to bring her little 5-year-old daughter to luncheon. When she saw the Queen eating the leg of a quail with her fingers, the child pointed an accusing finger at her, exclaiming in shocked tones: 'Piggy-wiggy! Oh, Piggy-wiggy!'

*   *   *   *   *

In the rebellious climate of modern times the food in educational establishments is not an uncommon deterrent to attendance. One morning, after refusing to eat his breakfast, a son told his mother that nothing would make him attend school that day. When asked why, he replied: 'I have many reasons for staying away – I detest the boys and they detest me and the school meals aren't fit for pigs!'

Mother responded: 'I can give you two far better reasons for going – you are fifty-two and you are their headmaster.'

*   *   *   *   *

129

Great Dining Disasters

Godfrey Winn in *The Infirm Glory* remembers what happened one afternoon after lunch when he was a child poring over a picture-book in the drawing-room while his father snoozed and his mother enjoyed a second cup of coffee. He happened to let his mouth fall wide open and the next moment his observant, fond mother jumped up and rushed over to him and stared with growing alarm into the gap. To her horror, all she could see was a dark, brown tunnel. She had been worrying for some time about the boy's backwardness in learning to talk. So he wasn't mentally retarded, but had no roof to his mouth!

Rousing her husband, she told him what she had discovered and off they went to call on the doctor and seek his advice. After examining Godfrey, he smiled and said: 'Dear lady, your son has a perfectly good roof to his mouth, but at the moment it is concealed by a thick layer of unmasticated chocolate!'

The offending artichoke

Frank Case had a hard time trying to keep solvent when he started the Algonquin Hotel in New York. It soon became the home of thespians and authors beginning their careers, but Case's own troubles were worsened because they were always short of cash, and, having a kind heart, he allowed their unpaid bills to pile up. One young playwright, who later became world-famous, lived and fed at the hotel for weeks without paying a cent. Evon when the total debt reached $2000, Case took no action because he believed in his guest's so-far-unrecognized talent.

Then, one evening, when Frank was feeling extremely despondent due to harassment from the hotel's creditors, he went into the dining-room, where he found the fellow enjoying the most expensive delicacy on the bill of fare, an artichoke. Such abuse of his indulgence infuriated Case, who rushed up to the offender's bedroom, had his bed removed and his belongings packed and taken down to the hall, then told him to clear out of the hotel.

The playwright took it all philosophically, and, as security for his debt, he handed Case the manuscript of a many-times-rejected work. The hotel owner, after reading it, persuaded Eugene Walter to 'doctor' it in exchange for 75 per cent of any future royalties. The play, when eventually produced, proved a hit under the title of *Fine Feathers*, but Case had to go to law to get his quarter share and was attacked in court as a grasping hotel-keeper who preyed upon creative artists.

Frank Case remained in charge of the Algonquin until he died in June 1946, and its continued success was a tribute to his genius as a hôtelier.

William Faulkner, the novelist, made it his home. One evening after a meal, he looked ill. 'My stomach is bothering me,' he complained.

Case nodded and said: 'Something you wrote, no doubt.'

Indian pudding

That much-married comedian De Wolf Hopper used to stay at the Algonquin whenever he had a Broadway engagement. While there he would press his wife to partake of his favourite Indian pudding. As he made his entrance through the dining-room curtains, Hopper's expressive eyebrows would be raised in the direction of George, the head waiter, who would nod if the dish were available. Then the actor would beam happily, and before sitting down he would visit all the other tables in turn extolling the mouth-watering merits of the pudding and urging the amused clientèle to try it.

Alexander Woollcott has related how only on one occasion did anyone dare to demur, and this was when Raymond Hitchcock rasped that he thought rice pudding far superior. Hopper stared incredulously at him for a moment before embarking on a tirade full of scorn for a man who would choose so common a dish when the divine Indian pudding was on the menu.

Enfeebled by the other's verbal volleys, Hitchcock, to placate him, ordered Indian pudding, and, with the ecstatic look of a hot-gospeller gaining a convert, Hopper then started on his own meal. But clearly he ate only to stimulate his appetite for that dish of dishes that was to follow.

'Now, George,' he said at length, 'bring me the Indian pudding.'

The minutes mounted without George returning, then, at last, losing his composure for the first time in his waiting career, he tottered into the room and told the impatient comedian: 'I'm sorry, Mr Hopper, but we have just served the last portion to Mr Hitchcock.'

Many a slip

The captain of the *Ile de France*, asked for his most nerve-wracking experience when crossing the Atlantic, replied that it occurred on the final evening of a voyage, when as customary he dined with the first-class passengers. The gastronomic masterpiece the head chef had created for the dinner was described on the menu as Turbot Soufflé Surprise.

In the liner's kitchen, the cooked turbot was being taken on a dish by the *commis* to the fish chef for dressing with the sauce when the youth stumbled and the turbot slid on to the floor, where it disintegrated, leaving only the head and tail whole. As they were serving fillet of sole to the tourist class, the chef overcame the crisis by carefully retrieving the head and tail of the turbot, setting them on another large dish and adding in between some of these sole fillets, trimmed to the correct outline. Next, he laid mushroom purée on top, followed by more fillets, and lastly he made quite sure that the shape was identical to that of a fine turbot before sending it to the sauce chef, who drenched the substitute with the sauce intended for the real thing.

The dining-room staff in the meantime were becoming increasingly concerned about the delay, but were calmed by a message that it was deliberate, for, as the *plat's* name implied, it had to be finished just before serving. When the great moment came and portions of Turbot Soufflé Surprise lay on their plates, delighted gasps came from the gastronomes, who prided themselves on their palates. Ecstatic exclamations of approval followed as they ate.

Despite such success, the fish chef refused to serve the dish ever again, not wishing to tempt Providence.

*　*　*　*　*

A similar disaster occurred at a banquet given by Talleyrand in honour of the Tzar. An enormous, ostentatiously decorated salmon was carried into the dining-hall by a waiter, who then dropped it on to the floor. The gourmet diplomat signalled to another waiter, who went and came back at once bearing another, its twin in size and adornment. The

incident had been prearranged by the wily Frenchman so as
to impress the Russian ruler.

*   *   *   *   *

A certain London hostess giving a dinner also proved equal
to the occasion when a footman slipped while carrying in a
superb tongue and let it fall to the floor.

She looked down at it and said with a smile: 'What a
lapsus linguae!' Everybody laughed at her wit. However,
among the guests was an uneducated woman who did not
really know what the Latin phrase meant. None the less,
impressed by the mirth it had aroused, she decided to make
the same comment when she had a dinner party. She asked
the footman to pretend to stumble on entering and let a
choice ham fall off the dish he carried. He did so, and she
duly cried: 'What a *lapsus linguae!*' No one laughed, and she
could not understand why.

*   *   *   *   *

Even worse than dropping dishes is spilling soup over
guests. Lord Coleridge in his reminiscence recalls that in
July 1891 such an indignity befell the Archbishop of York,
whereupon the prelate looked round the table and asked:
'Will any layman express my feelings?'

A clumsy waiter once spilt a full cup of black coffee all
over Beatrice Lillie's costly evening gown. The actress had
the wit and presence of mind to tell him: 'Go – and never
darken my Dior again!'

*   *   *   *   *

Waiting is not normally a dangerous occupation, but on one
occasion a nervous young waiter found himself in hospital
after being knocked out by an outraged husband. The boy
had spilt a dish of peas down the front of his wife's low-cut
evening gown and then groped with his fingers to try to
retrieve them.

*   *   *   *   *

Men can also suffer at the hands of clumsy waiters, but it can be swiftly forgiven and forgotten if an *amende honorable* is made. The writer Joseph Wechsberg was dining in a packed *trattoria* in Rome when a waiter fell and spilled a full bottle of red Barolo all over the trousers of his new grey suit. He was drenched to the skin from the waist downwards.

The owner of the place rushed up, seized hold of Wechsberg and hurried him into the kitchen, where he asked him to take off his trousers. Then, with tablecloths tied round his waist, Wechsberg returned to his table where he feasted on *spaghetti alla carbonara* and, as a peace offering, a bottle of Barolo. Finally, he was requested to go back to the kitchen where he found his trousers washed, dried and ironed.

Michael Wilding, in his autobiography *Apple Sauce*, describes a similar experience, but in his case it occurred in his youth when he was acting as a waiter. Each year the Duke of Windsor, when Prince of Wales, used to visit Christ's Hospital where Michael was a boarder. After the Prince had addressed the boys and was being escorted to the dining-room, Michael, although it was not his day for serving at table, dashed into the kitchen and begged the chef to let him take the Prince his soup. The chef handed him a silver tray loaded with plates of soup for everyone at the high table.

Proud but very nervous, the boy carried the tray into the dining-hall. He had almost reached his goal when he slipped on the polished floor and fell over, soup-soaked to the skin. The Headmaster gave him a murderous look, but the Prince, in complete contrast, called out so that everyone could hear: 'Don't worry, dear boy. At home I always skip the soup anyway.'

* * * * *

Even the most experienced waiters cannot always avoid spilling the soup when aboard a lurching ocean liner. Such a mishap happened as a quick-witted waiter was serving an obviously queasy diner. 'Don't worry, madam,' he said soothingly, first making as if to wipe round her mouth, 'it could happen to anyone.'

When food isn't what it seems

It is never a good idea to leave anything on your table in a restaurant, even if you are only leaving the room for a short while. An hotel in Birmingham had an auction-room next door where rare bulbs were sold. One lunch-time a man who had bought some was examining them when he was called to the telephone. He left behind on the table three tulip bulbs, the skins of which had fallen off. In his absence, a man who had already drunk several pints of beer sat down at the table for a snack and when the waiter passed he told him: 'I don't think much of your onions, Tom. I much prefer them pickled.'

The waiter could not understand what the man meant, for he had not put out any onions, but he made no comment as he was busy serving drinks. Then the bulb-fancier returned to discover that the beer-drinker had eaten them in mistake for onions: some of his friends had witnessed this from a nearby table and been much amused to see him dipping the tulip bulbs in salt.

*   *   *   *   *

Mice, too, should be careful what they eat. Cecil Roberts in *Sunshine and Shadows* recalls that when he had an honorary LL.D. conferred on him by the Washington and Jefferson College he received a parchment scroll, which he kept in its carton. Then, five years later during a clearance, he picked the carton up and heard something rattle inside it. Inside, he found a petrified mouse. Of the parchment only a few nibbled inches remained. The mouse had consumed it and been killed by the arsenic with which vellum is dressed.

'As there was no method of extracting my degree from the mouse's stomach,' says Roberts, 'I therefore bottled the petrified container.'

He kept this on his mantelpiece and when friends asked about this macabre ornament he explained that it was his LL.D. degree.

When food isn't what it seems

*   *   *   *   *

The short-sighted can court confusion if, through vanity or forgetfulness, they leave off their glasses. A myopic star of the English stage attended a dinner in honour of a celebrated French actress who was visiting London. After the preliminary cocktails and canapés, the guests went into the dining-room. Dame X squinted at something small and red on the great Parisienne's bodice, then she whispered, 'Darling, a piece of pimento has dropped off a canapé. Shall I remove it for you?'

'*Certainement non!*' replied the other in frigid tones. 'That is the ribbon of the *Légion d'Honneur*.'

The late Bernard Newman, probably the most sought-after lecturer of his day, recalled that once at a ladies' luncheon club the chairman, introducing him to the gathering, pointed at the red ribbon of the *Légion d'Honneur* in his buttonhole and said: 'It is most gallant of Mr Newman to keep this engagement when he's just been vaccinated.'

Embarrassing encounters

Meeting an old flame in a restaurant when you are with your wife or your mother can produce a certain degree of discomfort. Lord Alington was once dining out with his strait-laced parent when Tallulah Bankhead came in with a friend. As they passed, the peer hurriedly looked the other way. Presently, that most uninhibited of actresses left her table and, going over to her former lover, asked huskily: 'Don't you recognize me, darling, with my clothes on?'

* * * * *

In her seventies, the celebrated Rosa Lewis of the Cavendish Hotel in Jermyn Street caused much embarrassment to the managements of the Ritz and Hyde Park hotels when her own was bomb-damaged during the Second World War and she went to dine in their grill rooms and restaurants. Anthony Masters in his book *Inside Marble Halls* records that she insisted on speaking to the people at all the other tables and was unmerciful if she recognized them as former customers of her own – and unbearably rude if she didn't.

'How's the old water works? Still as unreliable as ever?' she called to a duke, whilst an ancient marquess was greeted with 'Hallo, mutton chops – still fancy a nice clean whore?' and an old military man with 'Hallo, droopy drawers, when are you coming round to the Cavendish to bounce a cheque?' A senior officer in the Guards almost died of apoplexy when she asked him if he still got 'the lover's droop'.

Rosa Lewis took with her to the Hyde Park, where she resided for a time, her West Highland terrier, Kippy. One day Mary Shiffer, the grill-room waitress, trod on the dog and spilt some tomato soup on the tablecloth. Rosa shrieked: 'You careless bitch – mind my bleeding dog!'

A slanging match instantly erupted.

'Who do you think you are coming in here, calling people names, making dirty cracks, embarrassing our gentlemen?' Mary demanded.

138

'Gentlemen! There are no bloody gentlemen here!' Rosa retorted.

'And you're no lady. Why don't you go back to your – to your tarts' paradise?' scoffed the other.

'If I did, I'd take half your clients with me – the lot probably!' Rosa railed.

Then the air-raid siren sounded and the dispute ceased as everyone hurried down into the shelters.

That evening Mrs Lewis packed. Before leaving the hotel, she sought Mary out and put a £5 note in front of her. Then, ignoring the waitress's rejection of the money, she went off in a taxi – back to the Cavendish.

* * * * *

It can be very awkward to be discovered enjoying lunch at a restaurant by someone who knows you ought to be at another function. This was what happened at the Ritz to the 21-year-old Oswald Mosley. Lady Cunard went up to him and asked: 'Were you not being married five minutes ago?'

With a gasp he jumped up and raced, leaving his hat behind, down St James's Street to the Chapel Royal where his bride, Lady Cynthia Curzon, was wondering what had happened to him.

* * * * *

In the days before the law against soliciting stopped the ladies of the town from parading out of doors in search of business, a visitor to London was walking up and down Bond Street looking at the shop-window displays. He was killing time before he went to meet his wife at the chiropodist's where she was having her corns removed. An attractive blonde kept following him, and told him that she had a room just round the corner where for £10 she could give him one hour of bliss. At first he took no notice, then he told her that he had only £2 on him as he hadn't been to the bank. She moved off.

Half an hour later the tourist, having collected his wife, was having a light lunch with her in a café when the blonde came in. On passing their table, she stared searchingly at the wife and scoffed: 'See what you get for two quid!'

Great Dining Disasters

*   *   *   *   *

At a reception following a concert held in London's Festival Hall in honour of Sir Robert Mayer's 100th birthday, Lady Diana Cooper spoke to a very amiable little woman who clearly knew her well but whom she herself did not at first recognize. Then, as she noticed what superb jewellery the other was wearing, Lady Diana became uncomfortably aware that she had been talking to the Queen. To make amends she forced her arthritic limbs into a deep curtsey and blurted out in apology: 'Ma'am, oh, ma'am, I'm sorry, ma'am – I didn't recognize you without your crown.'

Queen Elizabeth II's reply showed admirable quick wit: 'It was so much Sir Robert's evening that I decided to leave it behind.'

The waiting game

If you are fed up with being a waiter and want to make yourself as unpopular as possible with the wretched customers during your last week, what could you do? Well, there are old jokes that you might act out in real life with variations, or you might be inspired into making some rapier-sharp ripostes of your own.

For example, if after vainly trying to attract your attention for twenty minutes, a would-be customer jumps up and demands to see the owner, adding, 'I have a complaint', give him a pitying look and reply: 'This is a restaurant, sir – not a hospital.'

Or, if it's very late, you might at last go to him and say: 'Would you please pay your bill, sir? We're closing now.'

He will, of course, protest that he has not yet been served, to which you will answer. 'Then there'll only be the cover charge.'

But to get rid of a customer so soon would deprive you of much sport and obliterate your chances of gaining the 'Worst Waiter of the Year' award. You approach him with a bored expression and your thoughts clearly elsewhere. 'Where's the menu?' he demands urgently.

You: 'Down the stairs, two doors to the right.'

'The bill of fare!' he thunders. You depart in leisurely search of one.

'Is there any soup on this?' he asks, putting on his glasses.

You: 'There was but I wiped it off.' You set down a plate before him.

He, after tasting the *potage maison*: 'This isn't fit for a pig!'

You: 'I'll take it back and bring you some that is.' You do so.

He: 'Horrible – why, the stuff tastes like dish-water.'

You: 'How do you know?'

Next course. 'What is this leathery stuff?'

You: 'That, sir, is fillet of sole.' This time the diner wins the duel of words: 'Take it away and see if you can't get me a nice tender piece from the upper part of the boot.'

But you win with the steak. The man, exhausted by his efforts, says: 'Take this back, too, and bring me another well-beaten with a mallet. I can't even begin to cut it.'

Great Dining Disasters

You, after closely examining the reject: 'Sorry, sir. Can't swop this. You've bent it!'

During the festive season. 'This turkey isn't as good as what I had here a year ago.'

You: 'It ought to be, sir. It's come off the same turkey.'

For sweet, the fellow selects apple pie. 'Waiter, there's soap in this!'

You: 'It's to wash down the food.'

Then, when you serve him coffee, he says it tastes like cocoa. You: 'Oh, I'm sorry, sir, I've brought you a melted ice cream.'

This nuisance now complains that when he last came in the portions served him were twice as large. You: 'Where were you sitting?'

He: 'Over there by the window.'

You: 'Oh, that was for attracting customers.'

The sap persists: 'You advertised that this restaurant is under new management, but I saw the same manager peer through the service hatch just now.'

You: 'Yes, sir, but he got married yesterday.'

If you don't want to be bothered, because you are the only waiter left on duty, you might try putting cards in the window with some discouraging message. For example: 'In a hurry? Then why not have a coffee and roll downstairs?' Ambiguous, of course, but what does it matter? Or: 'Do you want yesterday's chef's special or today's? If today's, you'll have to come back tomorrow.' Or: 'At our restaurant parties up to 300 can and have been done.' Or: 'Don't stand outside and look miserable. Come inside and be fed up.' Or: 'Marriage is like this restaurant: you take what looks good to you and pay for it later.' Or: 'All our cups are cracked, and we have saucers to match.' Or: 'There is a £5 deposit on the stomach pump.' And, a warning: 'No dissatisfied customer is ever allowed to leave the premises.'

You may get a phone call later from an irate customer complaining that the food you served has given him the worst attack of indigestion he ever had. You might reply: 'I'm very glad to hear that, sir. Our patrons who are gourmets like to have such an after-effect so that they can have a dose of their favourite medicine. Without that, half the pleasure of eating is gone.'

142

*   *   *   *   *

A splendid model for those seeking this award might be the waiter encountered by E. King of Frinton-on-Sea and his party. Writing in *Signature*, the magazine of the Diners' Club, he described the gala opening of a luxury hotel in Australia. Tickets were both rare and costly. Mr King and eleven others sat patiently for an hour, feeling increasingly hollow inside and sweltering in the heat of high summer. At last, a waiter threw down a heap of cutlery before him, saying: 'Pass 'em down, cobber. Fish is first. Soup's not 'ot yet.'

Eventually even the worst waiter must leave this world. How can this paragon maintain his unpopularity? The widow of one, hoping to get into touch with him, attended a séance. Suddenly, there was impatient knocking. 'Mike!' she exclaimed. 'Darling – is that you? Talk to me, please!'

Mike's voice replied. 'I can't. It's not my table.'

The rebellious customer

If you are a customer vainly seeking service in a restaurant, pangs of hunger may spur you to sarcasm when the waiter does condescend to approach. Whether this achieves the desired punitive effect is doubtful, but at least it vents your spleen. You may be so proud of your remarks that you will boast about them later to friends, only to be told that one of their ancestors said the same thing umpteen years ago.

For those who have poor memories or only dream up suitable verbal coals of fire the day after, here are some ways in which the dissatisfied have expressed their feelings in the past. At last, the waiter arrives and says: 'We have everything on the menu, sir.'

You, staring distastefully at the grubby list: 'So I see. What about a clean one?'

You, twenty minutes later, calling: 'Are you the waiter who took my order?'

He nods.

You: 'Still looking well, I see. How are your grandchildren?'

Waiter: 'Your fish will be coming in a minute or two now, sir.'

You: 'What bait are you using?'

Or, if in a hurry, you might go straight to the meat course. You: 'Waiter, an hour ago I ordered some lamb chops. Have you forgotten them, or have I eaten them? Or are you waiting to hijack a lorry?'

Suppose you are flush and order something extravagant: 'Waiter, there's no claw on my lobster. Why is that?'

He explains: 'Well, sir, they are so fresh that they fight each other in the kitchen.'

You: 'Take this one away, and bring me one of the winners.'

(This joke has also been used for a spring chicken substituting 'leg' for 'claw'.)

If your chicken has two legs, you might find it a *pièce de resistance* as far as your knife and fork are concerned.

You: 'This must be an incubator chicken.'

The waiter asks why.

You: 'No chicken with a mother could be so tough.'

144

The rebellious customer

Of course, it might be mother causing you to complain: 'Why, it's nothing but skin and bones!' Once when I said this, a red-faced boor at the next table remarked to his blonde date with a guffaw: 'What does he want on it? Feathers!'

*   *   *   *   *

When Nicole, Duchess of Bedford, in her days as a television producer, wished to acquire the rights to base a series on some Sherlock Holmes stories, she arranged to meet the author's son, Dennis Conan Doyle, and his wife, Nina, for lunch at the Trianon Palace Hotel at Versailles, but failed to arrive until the cheese course. The supercilious *maître d'hôtel* took no notice of her for some time then, when he did, declared that everything except cold meat was off. The Duchess replied that she needed something hot and he reluctantly offered to get her some steak. Inwardly seething at such treatment in a de luxe hotel, she managed to force a smile and told him to inform the chef that her steak must be cut from between the fourth and fifth ribs of a young steer, charred outside and left raw within.

The *maître d'hôtel* solemnly noted down these requirements. Then the Duchess added: 'Before I eat the meat, I want to see it, so will you please present it to me?'

Eventually, the man returned bearing a silver dish, the lid of which he removed with a flourish. Nicole noticed that the chef was watching from the kitchen doorway. Giving the steak but a cursory glance she said: 'Now chop it up and give it to my dog.'

*   *   *   *   *

Women are in many ways far braver than men. A housewife once asked for some roast beef to be cut off the joint for her at a delicatessen.

'How much do you want?' asked the owner.

'Start cutting,' commanded the customer.

After he had assembled several slices before her, he paused, enquiring: 'Sufficient?'

She shook her head and urged: 'Go on cutting – go on!'

At last, she cried: 'Stop! I'll have those last two slices that have got no fat on them.'

Great Dining Disasters

*   *   *   *   *

Customers tired of being served skimpy portions might try, if they have sufficient nerve, the prank played by the comedian Jack Pearl on Lindy's of New York. Having bought in advance some of the best corned beef and hidden it in his pocket, he sat down at a table in the restaurant and ordered a corned-beef sandwich. On being served this, he stealthily added what he had purchased to it. Then he asked to see the head waiter and said: 'How can you afford to give me so much prime beef in a single sandwich?'

The man examined the packed sandwich, calculated in his mind the cost of all that meat, and marched rapidly towards the kitchen with a grim look that boded ill for the staff there.

*   *   *   *   *

When one finds a first-rate restaurant, it is wise to frequent it as much as possible lest the day come when, after you have dwelt in a gourmet's paradise thanks to the soup and the entrée, you are without warning flung into hell by the vile pudding and coffee, through a new management having taken over in the middle of the meal.

Greasing the palm

Tipping can embarrass both those who are expected to give and those who hope to receive. A mean millionaire was asked why he stayed at a certain resort right to the end of the season. He replied: 'I couldn't afford to leave while there were so many servants to tip. I had to remain until most of them were gone.' Asked the difference between courage and discretion, a politician who crossed the Atlantic frequently in the 1920s replied that to travel on an ocean liner without tipping would be courageous, and to return on another ship would be discreet.

After staying as paying guests in the historic castle of an English duke, the spokesman of some American tourists told the butler, 'I'm afraid I've made a bloomer. I tipped His Grace instead of you.'

The butler's face fell as he murmured: 'Now I'll never get it.'

Attempts to end tipping have not proved too successful. One restaurant had a notice on the wall that said, 'Please do not insult our waitresses by tipping them.' But on the tables were boxes with coin slots marked 'INSULTS'. When a customer nevertheless remarked: 'I see that tips are forbidden', a waitress told her: 'So were the apples in the Garden of Eden.'

Where the service provided by the staff is deplorable even the most generous of customers can refuse to hand out gratuities. An affluent author staying in a New York hotel was so dissatisfied that he decided to tip no one on departure. He had successfully slipped out unnoticed and was going down the steps to his car when the head waiter came running after him with palm outstretched and called: 'You're going to forget me, sir?'

The other seized the proffered hand and shook it: 'Oh, no, I shall write to you, of course.'

*   *   *   *   *

Children often make pertinent comments on the behaviour of grown-ups. The head waiter from an exclusive restaurant took his little daughter to the zoo. They happened to pass the

147

lion-house just when the keeper hurled in an enormous piece of raw meat, nearly hitting the beast, then moved off without a backward glance. 'How rude!' exclaimed the girl. 'Why didn't the man serve it to Mr Lion in the way you do, daddy?' she asked.

'That's because he knows he won't get a tip,' her father told her.

*   *   *   *   *

Shish kebab, a speciality of the celebrated Pump Room in Chicago, was always served with great panache. The waiter would rush into the restaurant from the kitchen bearing the lamb on a flaming sword held high in the air. 'What the heck is that?' asked Doris Day when she was dining there one evening with Jimmy Durante, and he replied: 'A customer who only left a $10 tip.'

Welshing customers

Restaurant dinners can sometimes cost the proprietors themselves dear. That notorious dabbler in black magic, Aleister Crowley, was an habitué of London's Café Royal, but the time came when he decided to seek new pastures. He chose the occasion of his birthday for the final farewell, inviting many friends and acquaintances to a party where, regardless of expense, vintage champagne flowed. Then, slipping out into Regent Street, he made off without paying the bill and never returned.

*   *   *   *   *

Sometimes quite the reverse happens. Once the last remaining customer in a Montmartre café was still slumbering at his table when the clock struck 3 am. 'Time you throw out that old drunk,' the cleaning woman said to the owner, 'You've already woken him four times. Shall I help you to get rid of him?'

'Don't you dare touch him,' he replied. 'Every time I rouse him, he asks for his bill and pays it.'

*   *   *   *   *

Among O. Henry's many short stories is a little-known one, believed to be based on a true incident, called 'The Venturers'. It opens with two grey-haired men sitting on a park bench in New York towards mid-day in summer. Both are looking admiringly at the hotel facing them. 'Beautiful, isn't it?' one remarks. 'D'you know, I'd rather fancy eating a good lunch in its roof garden today. There's a slight drawback, however: I haven't a cent on me.'

'That's odd,' replied the other. 'Neither have I.' He pondered for a moment or two, then he went on: 'I have a suggestion to make. Both of us look respectable enough. Let's go up to that roof garden and order the fanciest food and wines on the menu. Then, just before the check comes, we'll borrow a coin from a waiter, and toss to see who walks out a free man and who stays to face the music.'

The plan was agreed and the two men enjoyed a delicious

149

lunch. At last one said, studying the check: 'Look here, my friend, I'm afraid I'm guilty of having misled you. When I told you over in the park that I didn't have a cent with me, it was true. But please stop worrying about this large check. I'm worth a mint. I simply forgot to transfer my belongings when I put on my new suit this morning. Fact is, I must confess, I occupy the most expensive suite in the place!'

'I guess that makes us even,' laughed the other man. 'I should have recognized you. I own this hotel.'

*   *   *   *   *

Honoré de Balzac, the great French novelist, once invited his publisher, Werdet, to lunch at a paradise for wealthy gourmets, the restaurant Véry in the Palais Royal. According to Werdet's account, he himself had acute gastritis and could hardly eat anything while the author of *La Comédie humaine*, who had a huge appetite, consumed a hundred Ostend oysters, a dozen lamb cutlets, a duckling with turnips, a brace of roast partridges, a sole *à la normande*, *hors d'oeuvres* and dessert, all washed down with wines, coffee and liqueurs.

When Balzac had finished feasting, he asked Werdet in a whisper: 'Have you any money?' The publisher bent down and, making as if he had picked up a 5-franc coin from the floor which Balzac must have dropped, he handed it to him. The novelist signalled to the waiter for the bill, wrote something across the bottom of it, and tipped the fellow with the 5 francs. Then, Honoré rose with imposing aplomb and went out with his guest, who could not resist enquiring what he had written on the bill, and received the answer: 'You'll find out tomorrow.'

Next morning, a messenger from Véry's called on the publisher at his office and produced the bill, which totalled no less than 62 francs 50 centimes and on which Balzac had written: 'M. Werdet will be pleased to settle this account if presented at his office in the morning.'

*   *   *   *   *

Down on his luck in New York trying to earn a living as a liquor salesman, David Niven had failed to pull off a deal at a bar when a short, fat man, somewhat ridiculously dressed as a cowboy, turned awkwardly away from the counter so that his spurs got entangled and he fell into Niven's arms. They became friendly and the man, Doug Hertz, who lived on his wits, taught the future film star his cheap eating plan.

A big, busy restaurant near 48th Street was chosen. Niven went in by himself, found a vacant table and ordered a coffee and a doughnut. After a few minutes, Hertz entered and sat at the same table and ordered soup, steak, potatoes, pie and coffee. They behaved like complete strangers. Niven read a newspaper, sipped at a second cup of coffee and took his time finishing the doughnut.

Once Hertz had ceased eating, he asked the waitress for his check and Niven did the same. She slammed them down on the table, then, once she was out of the way, Hertz seized Niven's bill, made for the cashier, paid and left. Meanwhile, Niven continued studying his paper, and after a while he reached out for Hertz's account, stared at it in assumed dismay and called urgently for the waitress. He had never been served all this expensive steak and dessert, only coffee and a doughnut.

The girl conferred with the manager and the latter with the cashier, but they could not make a customer pay for what he had not been given. A fresh check was prepared which Niven settled and then, no doubt taking care to ensure that he was not tailed, he left and rejoined Hertz at a distant pre-arranged street corner. A second crowded restaurant was chosen where roles were reversed with Hertz ordering coffee and doughnut and Niven enjoying a steak dinner.

A cod-piece for the audience

When John Barrymore was appearing on the New York stage in *Redemption*, it was winter and most of his audiences seemed to be in the throes of bronchitis. This so got on the star's nerves that he decided to teach them a lesson. One evening the coughing during the first act was almost continuous. It started up again the moment he reappeared in the second act, but he was armed for action. Without warning, he whipped out a 5-lb cod from under his coat and hurled it over the footlights. 'Stop your gullets with this, you damned walruses!' he shouted. 'And let us get on with the play!'

It was a bonus those attending the play did not relish and its smell acted as a cough-deterrent for the rest of the performance.

The morning after

Excessive liquid intake at a social function can have some strange consequences. Once John Barrymore and Richard Bennett were staying at the same hotel. Bennett woke in his hotel bedroom the morning after a night of over-indulgence feeling as if his skull had been battered by a hammer.

When at last able to think, he wondered what had happened to Barrymore and picked up the receiver to phone him. He had difficulty getting through and shouted irritably into the mouthpiece: 'Hello – hello!'

'Hello,' Barrymore's drowsy voice replied.

'Are you OK?'

'Sure. What about you?'

'The same. Couldn't get you. Are you in your room or in the lobby?'

'Don't know.'

'What d'you mean, you don't know?'

'It's very dark. Oh, now I can see daylight.'

And Barrymore's famous profile, looking like a travesty of itself, peered up at Bennett as he crawled from under the bed.

* * * * *

Gilbert Miller, the theatrical manager, once gave a lavish dinner party at the Waldorf and a good deal of drinking went on after the meal. Presently, Helen Hayes went up to him and confided: 'Charlie [MacArthur, her husband] is a bit high and is having too much fun to leave now. I've got an early rehearsal tomorrow and want to slip away. Will you be a dear and see that he gets to bed OK?'

'Of course I will,' Miller assured Helen, and, once his guests had departed, he piloted Charlie to his car and pushed him into the back, where he promptly fell asleep. After driving him fifty miles to Nyack, the impresario was astonished to find the house boarded up and padlocked. Unable to get any coherent response from his passenger, he went back to New York, carried him into his own apartment and left him on a couch for the night.

Next morning, Miller received a frantic phone-call from

153

Great Dining Disasters

Helen. 'What have you done with Charlie?' she asked angrily. Gilbert told her about his fruitless journey.

'Oh, how remiss of me – but I thought you knew,' the star replied. 'We're living at the Waldorf for the winter.'

*   *   *   *   *

The 'morning after' begins, of course, any time after midnight. An MP and his wife were in bed following a dinner to celebrate their Silver Wedding anniversary when the telephone rang. The wife picked up the receiver. It was the Party Whip, who asked her to tell her husband that an unexpected and crucial vote was taking place in the House of Commons and he must rush back there at once. She roused him and passed on the message. Rebelliously, he muttered: 'Say, I'm not here.'

'My husband's not here,' she told the Whip, obediently.

Unfortunately for the MP, the Whip had overheard her husband's instructions.

'In that case, madam,' came the frigid reply, 'will you please tell the gentleman who is in bed with you to return here and vote?'

*   *   *   *   *

Other troubles can arise in the early hours of the morning after men, without their wives to restrain them, have drunk too much. Following a reunion dinner two friends living in the same vicinity zigzagged homewards along a road and eventually wandered through a gap in the hedge on to an abandoned branch line of British Railways. The man in front called to the other: 'Don't you find the shteps on these shtairs hellishly far apart?'

His pal agreed: 'Yesh, I do, but what's upsetting me is that the hand rail is so low.'

Eventually one of the revellers reached home, where, not surprisingly, he fell into a deep sleep, from which he was roused some hours later by his wife who accused him of having returned drunk. He protested innocence and told her that he could prove he had come home sober because he had found a young hedgehog in the outside lavatory and fetched it a saucer of milk.

154

The morning after

'So that's why I found that saucer next to the lavatory brush!' the wife exclaimed.

The lady vanishes

When, despite a warning from your horoscope, dining out has proved a delight and the *maître d'hôtel* is courteously bowing you out, it is still wise to watch your step. Bear in mind what happened to that star of the silent screen, Mabel Normand, who left a celebrated Hollywood restaurant in the early hours of the morning and found that a cloud-burst had left the sidewalk ankle-deep in mud. Her cavalier at once rose to the occasion by pulling off his new coat and flinging it down between her and the waiting Cadillac. In doing so, he burst the seam of his amply-waisted trousers, whilst Miss Normand, with a grateful smile, stepped elegantly forward – and vanished into a man-hole.

When rescued, Mabel might well have quipped: 'My exit is the result of too many entrées.'